D0440223

Peyton Manning: The Inspiring Story of One of Football's Greatest Quarterbacks

An Unauthorized Biography

By: Clayton Geoffreys

Copyright © 2017 by Calvintir Books, LLC

All rights reserved. Neither this book nor any portion thereof may be reproduced or used in any manner whatsoever without the express written permission. Published in the United States of America.

Disclaimer: The following book is for entertainment and informational purposes only. The information presented is without contract or any type of guarantee assurance. While every caution has been taken to provide accurate and current information, it is solely the reader's responsibility to check all information contained in this article before relying upon it. Neither the author nor publisher can be held accountable for any errors or omissions. Under no circumstances will any legal responsibility or blame be held against the author or publisher for any reparation, damages, or monetary loss due to the information presented, either directly or indirectly. This book is not intended as legal or medical advice. If any such specialized advice is needed, seek a qualified individual for help.

Trademarks are used without permission. Use of the trademark is not authorized by, associated with, or sponsored by the trademark owners. All trademarks and brands used within this book are used with no intent to infringe on the trademark owners and only used for clarifying purposes.

This book is not sponsored by or affiliated with the National Football League, its teams, the players, or anyone involved with them.

Visit my website at www.claytongeoffreys.com
Cover photo by Jeffrey Beall is licensed under CC BY 2.0 / modified from original

Table of Contents

Foreword 1

Introduction 3

Chapter 1: Childhood and Early Life 7

Chapter 2: College Years at the University of Tennessee.........12

    Freshman Year...13

    Sophomore Year..15

    Junior Year 16

    Senior Year 19

    Conclusion 22

Chapter 3: Peyton's NFL Career...............................23

    1998 NFL Draft 23

    Rookie Season 25

    1999 Season...28

    2000 Season...30

    2001 Season...32

    2002 Season...33

2003 Season..35

2004 Season..38

2005 Season..40

2006 Season..46

2007 Season..53

2008 Season..55

2009 Season..56

2010 Season..63

2011 Season..65

2012 Season..69

2013 Season..72

2014 Season..78

2015 Season..80

Retirement 87

Chapter 4: Manning vs. Manning............................91

Chapter 5: What Makes Peyton Manning So Great? 95

No-Huddle Offense 96

Peyton Works Hard Toward Everything 97

Chapter 6: Peyton's Obsessive Behavior 99

Chapter 7: Peyton's Bad Postseason Luck............................104

Most of the Games Were Fairly Close 106

His Teammates 106

The Broncos and Colts Have Terrible Playoff Records 107

Chapter 8: What is Next for Peyton? 109

Chapter 9: Peyton Manning's Legacy...........................111

Final Word/About the Author 114

References 117

Foreword

Peyton Manning has left a profound impact on the game of football. Since his days in Indianapolis to his time in Denver, Manning has cemented his iconic legacy as an all-time great quarterback. From consistently maintaining his composure in late game situations to upholding a classy reputation off the field, few football players have had the privilege of a long and sustained football career like Peyton Manning. His story is one of perseverance and determination. After we learn his backstory, we'll go into what personality traits make Peyton Manning so effective as a quarterback. We'll also review his postseason record and look ahead at what is next for the great Peyton Manning. This is easily one of the most fun football biographies I've had the pleasure of writing, due to the fact that Peyton Manning has had such an illustrious career. Thank you for purchasing *Peyton Manning: The Inspiring Story of One of Football's Greatest Quarterbacks*. In this unauthorized biography, we will learn Peyton Manning's incredible life story and impact on the game of football. Hope you enjoy and if you do, please do not forget to leave a review!

Also, check out my website at claytongeoffreys.com to join my exclusive list where I let you know about my latest books. To thank you for your purchase, you can go to my site to download a free copy of *33 Life Lessons: Success Principles, Career Advice & Habits of Successful People*. In the book, you'll learn from some of the greatest thought leaders of different industries on what it takes to become successful and how to live a great life.

Cheers,

Clayton Geoffreys

Visit me at www.claytongeoffreys.com

Introduction

While many will claim that various quarterbacks are the greatest of all time, no other name comes up more often than Peyton Manning. And nobody can argue that his record does not befit this status. He has won five NFL Most Valuable Player awards, the most by any player. He also currently holds the league records for most passing yards and most passing touchdowns. He runs a no-huddle offense like nobody's business. He was also able to turn around the Indianapolis Colts' losing ways after the growing pains he endured his rookie season. He has reached the postseason in all but two seasons, and he won two Super Bowls. Aside from Tom Brady and his five Super Bowl victories, it is hard to argue any other NFL quarterback can be considered the greatest of all-time except Peyton Manning.

Peyton Manning is acclaimed for harnessing a passion and competitiveness for the sport of football greater than anyone has ever seen. In fact, many believe that he is compulsively obsessed with winning. Growing up with his father Archie, who played professional football as a quarterback with the New Orleans Saints for most of his career, along with having two brothers who are also extremely passionate about football—Peyton was practically bred for the sport. Even at the early age of 3, Peyton was already learning how to throw a football. His younger brother, Eli Manning, is a professional quarterback for the New York Giants and also a two-time Super Bowl winner.

Football is in Peyton's blood, to say the least.

While Peyton has crushed many NFL previous records, he still could never be satisfied with his results. He always wants to become better. Anyone who knew Peyton on the field would classify him as being extremely obsessive about his goal of perfection on the football field. Peyton simply could never be content with his results, no matter his accomplishments.

Consider the fact he was sidelined for the entire 2011 season due to a neck injury. The doctors believed there was a high chance he would not be able to play professionally again at the age of 36. However, shortly after his surgeries, Peyton was back and ready to play. Many critics questioned whether he could be the same quarterback capable of making strong opposite-field throws and deep passes. Peyton proved them wrong by breaking some of the most important quarterback records in NFL history in his second season post-injury. Except for 2011, you saw him at every single game. He never missed one game while playing and even hated coming out with the outcome well in hand. Peyton was so passionate about football that nobody could beat his love for the sport.

Peyton was a brutal force against every defense in the NFL. He is considered one of the most knowledgeable NFL quarterbacks of all time. His extensive work in the film room allowed him to read opposing defenses, even disguised ones, in a few seconds at the line of scrimmage. If you rushed him, he knew how to get the ball out quickly. If he needed to make a comeback, he knew how to drive the ball and score. He was a real leader who brought out the best from all his offensive teammates, as nobody dared to come against the all-mighty Peyton Manning. If a player was not playing at his best, everyone knew that Peyton would let him know it, and they probably would not like what he would have to say.

That persona continued right up until his retirement after the 2015 season in which he left the NFL triumphant after the Denver Broncos defeated the Carolina Panthers to win Super Bowl 50. Much like the Broncos team president John Elway, who was himself a Hall of Fame quarterback and two-time Super Bowl winner as well as the man who brought Manning to the Mile High City, Manning left the game on his terms and at the top.

Peyton's love for the game teaches us the valuable lesson of what can be accomplished through hard work and dedication. While Peyton has the prototypical physique of an NFL quarterback, standing 6 feet 5 inches tall and able to throw laser-sharp throws to his intended receivers, Peyton's greatest strength is his intelligence. His intelligence was not something he was born with; he accomplished it through having one of the strongest work ethics that any quarterback has possessed. Nobody works harder than Peyton at playing at his best. Peyton Manning is completely self-motivated and driven toward becoming the best he can be. Because of that, he has not only achieved greatness as an NFL quarterback, but he brings the absolute best out of his entire team as well.

Through strong values and parents who showed him how to be extremely disciplined, Peyton was able to grow into the winning quarterback he is most remembered as. His parents taught him strong morals and always ensured that he would do the absolute best toward all of his disciplines. His father showed him everything he knew about football and instilled in him the most important steps toward being the absolute best he can be. Without the support of his family, he would not be what he is today.

If you would like to learn more about one of the greatest quarterbacks of all time, then read on! This book will go through Peyton's entire life. You will learn exactly what made Peyton the quarterback he is known for—the over-accomplisher. And you will learn how Peyton's obsession drives him toward his best and brings out the best in everyone around him.

Chapter 1: Childhood and Early Life

Peyton Manning was born on March 24, 1976. He has two brothers: Cooper, who is older than he is, and his younger brother, Eli. Peyton's father Archie had a football career that started when he was the quarterback for Ole Miss for three seasons – where he finished with 4,753 career passing yards and 30 touchdowns[i] – before being selected second overall by the New Orleans Saints in the 1971 NFL Draft. The elder Manning would play for the Saints between 1971 and 1982 and then later played for the Houston Oilers and Minnesota Vikings. Over his 13-year career, Archie Manning had respectable numbers with 23,911 passing yards and 125 touchdowns, though he also threw 173 career interceptions[ii]. Archie Manning's best season statistically was near the end of his run with the Saints in 1980 when he had 3,716 passing yards, 23 touchdowns, and 20 interceptions for a passer rating of 81.8, but the Saints went 1-15 that season.

Peyton grew up loving the game of football, and his father was his primary inspiration, which should be no surprise. Peyton began to learn how to throw a football when he was 3. In fact, the entire family loved football. They would often practice and compete against each other. Growing up, and even at an early age, Peyton had a dream of one day becoming a college quarterback star.

His older brother Cooper was considered one of the top receivers in the state of Louisiana before being recruited to play as a wide receiver at Ole Miss, following his father's footsteps. But in the first summer before Cooper's freshman season, he started to feel numbness down to his fingers and toes that led to him going to see specialists at the Mayo Clinic in Minnesota[iii]. There, he learned that he had spinal stenosis – a condition where the spine narrows and pinches the nerves. This would prevent the oldest Manning brother from continuing his football career.

Peyton recalls that his brother was a great player as well, and Cooper was someone that inspired him to become what he is today. Cooper drove the competitiveness within Peyton. Because Cooper was older than him, it would be difficult for Peyton to compete with him in his childhood years. However, this competitiveness would drive Peyton to want to become even better. The entire Manning family loved football and loved to compete, but Peyton had a compulsive competitiveness about him that drove him to become who he is today. Even at an early age, Peyton showed a competitive passion that even surpassed both of his brothers.

Peyton's parents taught their children the positive values that any good parents want their children to follow. They never pushed any of them into playing sports professionally, but they all naturally loved to play competitively. Peyton's parents always ensured that their children had a good education. This can be demonstrated by the fact that Peyton and his two brothers attended Isidore Newman School, which was one of the most prestigious prep college schools in New Orleans.

Peyton's father, Archie Manning, would often play tapes of his previous games and watch them with his children as they analyzed the defense. Archie recalls that Peyton, in particular, was practically mesmerized by watching the tapes, even at a very young age. As a teenager, Peyton would watch tapes for hours. His father was so surprised at how much tape Peyton would watch that he recommended his son to go "find a girlfriend" or do something else that a normal teenager would do. However, Peyton was insistent that he needed to watch the films so he could learn to become a great quarterback.

Peyton claims there was not a "secret formula" that led him to become the great quarterback we know. He said they were a typical family. However, it can be seen that they grew up with the right morals and work ethic. Archie would train his boys for hours. Since he now has two sons playing professional football at an elite level and at the sport's most demanding position, his hard work certainly paid off.

While Archie played for the Saints, they were often considered the laughingstock of the league because they lost many more games than they won. In 1982, Archie was traded to the Houston Oilers. Peyton was around six years old at the time. Archie and his wife decided that it would be best if she stayed in New Orleans with the children even though Archie would live in Houston while practicing and playing with his new team. This brought heartache to the family, as there would be long time periods in which they would not see their father.

Peyton dreamed of eventually playing football for an organized team, and he was able to do so in the seventh grade. When he was asked which positions he would like to play, he responded "Quarterback" and "Defensive Back," and thus Peyton became the team's quarterback.

Because Peyton spent a lot of time watching his father play football on the sidelines and studied his tapes, he was much more advanced in understanding the sport than all of his peers. He loved listening to audio tapes of his father's college football days. He became very knowledgeable and loved to quiz his family on them.

Even at an early age, Peyton was obsessed with competitiveness. He was far more competitive than his brothers. It was apparent, even at that young age, that he was destined to become a football legend. While he played other sports, nothing was more important to him than football, and he credits this love to his father, as he was inspired to play in the NFL, just like him.

An old janitor at Newman High School recalled the competitiveness of Archie and his three boys. He was required to work there on a work release while in prison, and he had to get to work at 4:30 in the morning. This janitor recalls that, when he arrived, he would see Archie, Cooper, and Peyton all practicing football on the field, even before the sun was up. He claimed that there was not a single day that he worked as a janitor that he did not see the three of them together practicing.

Peyton started at quarterback in his sophomore year. He led the team to a 34-5 record during the three seasons he played. Peyton wore the number 18 on his jersey out of respect for his older brother Cooper, who could no longer play football because he was diagnosed with spinal stenosis. Peyton was named the Gatorade Circle of Champions Player of the Year as a senior. His tremendous high school career made him one of the most sought-after quarterbacks in the nation. His brother Eli also wore the number 18 jersey, which has since been retired and is now hanging inside the school's gymnasium[iv].

Chapter 2: College Years at the University of Tennessee

Coming out of high school, Peyton was pursued by colleges across America. While there were many choices available, Peyton was continuously pressured to attend the University of Mississippi, the school that his father had played for. But Peyton was planning on making his legacy, and he thought he had a chance to succeed somewhere else in college football. Peyton shocked everyone when he decided to attend Tennessee, which was a Southeastern Conference rival of Ole Miss. While this upset many, his father learned that he had to accept his son's decision.

For Peyton, it was not just about football, but it was also about his education. He even placed his career on hold by making the stunning decision to stay in Knoxville for his senior season despite the fact he could have been taken No. 1 overall in the 1997 NFL Draft. Most star athletes who plan on playing professionally skip their senior years, since the NFL requires players to be three years removed from high school. Peyton did this so that he could receive his bachelor's degree with honors at the University of Tennessee. He then became arguably the best quarterback in school history. He threw for 11,201 yards and 89 touchdowns and won 39 of the 45 games he started. That broke the SEC record for career wins, among other memorable achievements.

Freshman Year[v]

When Peyton started at Tennessee, he was listed as the third-string quarterback and was expected to wait for his turn in later years to be the starting quarterback. However, the starting and second-string quarterbacks, Todd Helton and Jerry Colquitt, suffered injuries in his freshman year, which allowed Peyton to start in the fifth game of the season on October 1, 1994. Helton would later have a very productive baseball career with the Colorado Rockies, finishing as a five-time All-Star with more than 2,500 hits over a 17-year career.

The Volunteers started their season with a record of 1-3 with the lone win coming against the Georgia Bulldogs and the losses coming to UCLA, Florida, and Mississippi State. Manning took over during the Volunteers' 24-21 loss to Mississippi State on September 24, 1994.

Manning made his first career start at home against the Washington State Cougars the following week, producing a 10-9 win. That started a run in which Tennessee won six of its next seven regular-season games, a big turnaround from that disappointing start to the season. Tennessee defeated Arkansas 38-21 on October 8, 1994, before losing 17-13 to then-number 10 Alabama on October 15. That was the last loss that Manning and Tennessee suffered for a while, and they bounced back with a 31-22 win on the road against the South Carolina Gamecocks on October 29. The winning streak continued with a 24-13 win over the Memphis Tigers on November 12, a 52-0 shutout of the Kentucky Wildcats on November 19, and a 65-0 blowout of intrastate rival Vanderbilt on November 26. That final win remains Tennessee's largest win in the 125-year rivalry.

It was not a bad start to a collegiate football career, although Manning's numbers were relatively low. He completed 89 of 144 passes, a 61.8 completion percentage, for 1,141 yards, 11 touchdowns, and six interceptions. The Volunteers were focused more on their rushing attack since they were cautious with a freshman quarterback who had to take the reins of their offense much sooner than expected.

Tennessee's offense was led by senior running back James Stewart, who had 1,028 rushing yards and 11 touchdowns along with 147 receiving yards and three receiving touchdowns. Aaron Hayden was another senior running back who contributed 819 rushing yards and three touchdowns. Overall, the Tennessee rushing attack averaged 211.9 rushing yards and more than two touchdowns per game[vi].

Overall, Manning was building confidence, and the Volunteers ended the regular season 8-4. On December 30, the Volunteers played in the Gator Bowl where they defeated then-number 17 Virginia Tech 45-23. Manning had one of his better games of his freshman season, completing 12 of 19 passes for 189 yards against the Hokies.

At the end of the 1994 season, Manning was named to the Southeastern Conference's All-Freshman team and was also chosen as the SEC Freshman of the Year.

Sophomore Year[vii]

In the 1995 season, Peyton helped Tennessee win their first two games, 27-7, at home against East Carolina on September 2, and 30-27 over Georgia on September 9. The Volunteers had cracked the Top 10 in the polls, reaching number 8 after their fast start.

They won all of their remaining games except one, which was against the Florida Gators on September 16. As good as Manning played, and he played well with 326 passing yards and two touchdowns, Florida counterpart Danny Wuerffel had six TD passes and added a seventh rushing as Tennessee left "The Swamp" with a 62-37 loss despite holding a 30-21 halftime lead.

After Tennessee earned significant victories over Mississippi State (52-14) on September 23, and Oklahoma State (31-0) on September 30, Manning had another highlight performance on October 8, when the Volunteers defeated the 18th-ranked Arkansas Razorbacks by a score of 49-31. Against Arkansas, Manning completed 35 of 46 passes for 384 yards and one touchdown; it earned him national Player of the Week awards that were given out by the *Sporting News* and the U.S. Postal Service.

As the season continued, the Volunteers kept earning big wins, and Manning quickly climbed up the school's all-time passing list after throwing for 265 yards during Tennessee's 12-7 win over the Vanderbilt Commodores on November 25.

During the season, Manning had four 300-yard games, and seven games with at least two TD passes. Tennessee entered the Citrus Bowl on January 1, 1996, against Ohio State; the two teams shared the number 4 ranking nationally. The Volunteers defeated Ohio State, 20-14, with Manning connecting with star receiver Joey Kent on a 47-yard touchdown pass in the third quarter to break a 7-7 tie. But it was two field goals from Jeff Hall in the fourth quarter for 29 and 25 yards to help give Manning his second consecutive bowl game victory with the Volunteers.

Peyton finished sixth in the Heisman Trophy voting and was named to the second team on *College Sports Magazine*'s All-American list, as well as being on the Associated Press' All-American third team. In his sophomore season, Manning completed 244 of 380 pass attempts, setting school records with a 64.2 completion percentage and 2,954 passing yards. Manning also had 22 passing touchdowns against just four interceptions. The touchdown mark was only three short of the school record of 25 set by Heath Shuler in the 1993 season. Manning was already ranked fourth in school history in passing yards after two seasons.

Junior Year[viii]

Tennessee was ranked as the nation's second-best team behind Nebraska in the Associated Press pre-season polls, and the Volunteers were considered one of the odds-on favorites to compete for the national championship during the bowl season. They looked true to form in their two season-opening wins against non-conference opponents, starting with a 62-3 win over UNLV of the Western Athletic Conference. This was followed by a 35-20 win against Pacific Ten Conference squad UCLA on September 7.

The Volunteers suffered their first loss of the season on September 21 to the fourth-ranked Florida Gators, 35-29, in an early season showdown for SEC supremacy. Despite the heartbreaking loss, Manning set three separate school passing records, completing 37 passes of 65 attempts for 492 yards. He now held three of the school's seven major passing records. However, the Gators again got the better of him, as Manning also threw a career-high four interceptions. Tennessee bounced back quickly during a special Thursday night game on October 3, routing Ole Miss 41-3. The winning continued against the Georgia Bulldogs on October 12, a 29-17 win at home in which Manning had another 300-plus yard game. He completed 31 of 41 passes for 371 yards and two touchdowns. The game was unique because Manning completed a school-record 11 straight passes against the Bulldogs.

After the Volunteers earned a 20-13 win over the seventh-ranked Alabama Crimson Tide, they extended their winning streak on November 2 with a 31-14 win on the road against the South Carolina Gamecocks. Manning had one of his best games of the season, completing 27 of 36 for 263 yards with two touchdowns and was named Offensive Player of the Week in the SEC. Manning had more yards against the Memphis Tigers out of Conference USA with 296, but the Volunteers lost for the second time on November 9 by a score of 21-17.

It was a tough loss for the Volunteers, but they did not stay down long, as they won the final three games of their regular season. They had a 55-14 win over the Arkansas Razorbacks on November 16, a defeat of the Kentucky Wildcats by a score of 56-10 on November 23, and a 14-7 victory at arch-rival Vanderbilt on November 30.

After finishing second to Florida in the SEC Eastern Division for the second consecutive season, the Volunteers found themselves facing the two-time Big Ten Conference champions, the Northwestern Wildcats, in the 1997 Citrus Bowl played on January 1 at the Florida Citrus Bowl Stadium in Orlando, Florida. Manning was completely dominant in a 48-28 win over the Wildcats, completing 27 of 39 attempts for 408 yards and four touchdowns to receive the Citrus Bowl's Most Valuable Player award for the second consecutive year and his third straight bowl game win[ix]. His performance included a 43-yard pass to Peerless Price in the first quarter and a third-quarter pass to Joey Kent for 67 yards. Manning also had a 10-yard rushing touchdown as part of the 21-point first quarter. Northwestern attempted to make a comeback with 21 points of their own in the second quarter, which included two touchdowns by running back Darnell Autry.

Manning's junior stats included a 63.9 completion percentage, and he completed 243 of 380 pass attempts for 3,287 yards and 20 touchdowns. While he had more interceptions with 12, he still finished with a quarterback rating of 147.7 for the season and ended up eighth in the voting for the Heisman Trophy[x]. The award which went to Wuerffel, who led Florida's "Fun-n-Gun" offense with 3,625 passing yards, 39 touchdowns, and 13 interceptions his senior season[xi]. While Manning did not get a lot of votes in the Heisman Trophy race, he did earn a spot on the third-team All-American list through the Associated Press and *Football News* as well as being named to the All-SEC second team.

Senior Year[xii]

Peyton obtained his bachelor's degree in only three years. He could have gone into the NFL draft, in which he was projected to be a top pick in the first round. However, Peyton decided that he would play one more year with Tennessee, hoping that he could lead the Volunteers to a national championship. They started off on the right foot, ranked fifth in the nation, before a 52-17 rout of the Texas Tech Red Raiders of the Big 12 Conference on August 30. That was followed by a 30-24 win in Los Angeles the following week at UCLA.

However, the Volunteers once again lost to Steve Spurrier's Florida Gators – ranked third in the country at the time – by a 33-20 score on September 20. Tennessee then started a winning streak with a 31-17 victory over Ole Miss on October 4, a 38-13 win over 13th-ranked Georgia on October 11, and a 38-21 win over the Alabama Crimson Tide on October 18. Manning had 300 passing yards in each of the first six games as the Volunteers started 5-1. He passed for at least 300 yards in another three games in the second half of the season, including a dominant performance November 8 during a 44-20 win over the Southern Miss Golden Eagles – a game in which Manning threw for 299 yards and five touchdowns. Two weeks later on November 22, Manning had a collegiate career high of 523 passing yards to go with a career high-tying five touchdowns during a 59-31 win over the Kentucky Wildcats. Those were two of the four games in which Manning threw at least five touchdown passes.

After defeating the Vanderbilt Commodores on November 29, 1997, with a 17-10 decision at home, the Tennessee Volunteers finished their SEC schedule with a 7-1 record but won the Eastern Division because the Gators had suffered mid-season

Now the Volunteers faced off against the 11th-ranked and West Division champion Auburn Tigers in the SEC championship game, held on December 6, at the Georgia Dome in Atlanta. Long gone was the team that had lost to the Florida Gators. Manning threw a 40-yard touchdown pass to Peerless Price for an early 7-0 lead. But the Tigers showed their mettle by scoring the next 20 points, highlighted by a 51-yard pass from Auburn quarterback Dameyune Craig to receiver Tyrone Goodson. Manning threw a 46-yard touchdown pass to Price to make the score 29-23 in the final moments of the third quarter, followed by a 43-yard pass to Marcus Nash that gave Tennessee a 30-29 lead with 11:14 to play. They did not let go of that lead and won the 1997 SEC championship[xiii].

It was an impressive win for the Volunteers. They were ranked number 3 and accepted an invitation to the Orange Bowl on January 2, 1998, at Pro Player Stadium in Miami, Florida. But the Tennessee defense was unable to stop Ahman Green and Nebraska's vaunted wishbone running attack, and they lost the game. The Nebraska Cornhuskers were ranked second in the nation coming into the game and were undefeated after winning the Big 12 Championship. Nebraska continued their roll with a dominant win over Tennessee by a final score of 41-17. The Cornhuskers had 534 yards of offense, 409 of which came from their rushing game and 201 of which came from Green[xiv].

Nebraska led 28-3 in the third quarter before the Volunteers scored their first touchdown of the game on a 5-yard pass from Manning to Price. This was set up by their freshman running back Jamal Lewis having a 23-yard run as part of the 1,364 yards he had on the year. Overall, the Volunteers offense had just 315 total yards, with only 187 through the air. Manning did not finish the game, as sophomore backup Tee Martin threw a 3-yard pass to Andy McCullough for Tennessee's final touchdown.

With the Orange Bowl win, Nebraska shared the national championship with the Michigan Wolverines, who won the 1998 Rose Bowl by defeating the Washington State Cougars, 21-16. In the end, Manning had another great season with a completion rate of 60.2 percent (287 out of 477) for 3,819 yards while collecting 36 passing touchdowns against just 11 interceptions. His quarterback rating of

147.7 is still second-best among quarterbacks in SEC history. Any other year, Manning would have likely won the Heisman Trophy as the best player in college football but was second in the voting behind Michigan defensive back Charles Woodson, who led the nation with seven interceptions. Manning did receive the Johnny Unitas Golden Arm Award for his season while being named the Player of the Year by *Football News*.

Conclusion

Peyton Manning's success at Tennessee is still fondly remembered today, and it is visible to anyone visiting the school. Tennessee ended up retiring Peyton Manning's number 16. One of the streets leading to Neyland Stadium was renamed Peyton Manning Pass. That is the type of honor a quarterback receives when he finishes his four years of college football with a 39-5 record as a starter with the Volunteers[xv]. In addition to that, Manning owns almost all the single-game, season, and career records in school passing history. For his career, Manning completed 62.5 percent of his passes and had 11,201 passing yards with 89 touchdowns against 33 interceptions for a quarterback rating of 147.1 at Tennessee[xvi].

Peyton was not just remembered in Tennessee for his football career solely, but he is also exalted for his academic achievements as well. Anyone attending Tennessee quickly learns who Peyton is, and he will be remembered there for many years to come.

Chapter 3: Peyton's NFL Career

1998 NFL Draft

When it came to the 1998 NFL draft, there was only one other quarterback who could even remotely be considered as an alternative possible first overall pick, and that was Ryan Leaf. Leaf had played for the Washington State University Cougars, who lost in the 1998 Rose Bowl to Michigan in his senior season. He had a higher quarterback rating than Peyton Manning in his senior season at 158.7. For his career at Washington State, he passed for 3,968 yards, 34 touchdowns, and 11 interceptions[xvii]. Some felt that Ryan Leaf was a better alternative because Peyton Manning was so mechanical that he might not be able to adapt very well to the NFL, where the intensity would require him to be more naturally gifted in his decision-making.

However, many felt that Peyton was indeed the better quarterback, and the Indianapolis Colts ended up making Peyton the first overall selection. Of the six leading experts from *Sports Illustrated*, five believed that Peyton Manning should be considered as the first draft pick. The Colts had to determine whether they wanted Leaf or Manning as their quarterback. Ryan was known to have a better arm than Peyton, but both quarterbacks exhibited plenty of arm strength and could make every throw required of an NFL signal-caller. However, Peyton seemed to have a more mature outlook and seemed better-suited for playing in the NFL. Peyton went on the record as telling the Colts that if they wanted to win, they needed to make the right choice and draft him as their quarterback. Otherwise, they would have to play against him and face the consequences.

Jim Irsay, the owner of the Colts, contacted Leaf over the phone to speak about how they were leaning toward selecting Manning, who they felt was very polished. It was not very definite the evening before the draft in April 1998[xviii]. There were several late nights where the Colts' head coach Jim Mora and general manager Bill Polian pored over statistics, measurements, combine numbers, and other factors that were graded using a point system. Going number 2 did not seem to bother Leaf because he did not have a huge interest in playing for the Colts. In fact, he stated that he was more interested in playing for the San Diego Chargers, who had the second selection in the draft. The rest of the draft's top selection included the Arizona Cardinals selecting Florida State defensive end Andre Wadsworth, the Oakland Raiders picking Michigan safety and Heisman Trophy winner Charles Woodson, and the Chicago Bears going with Curtis Enis, a running back from Penn State.

Manning was going to join a team that hoped he could hit the ground running for a club that finished 1-15 in 1997, during which quarterback Jim Harbaugh was hit a lot and left lying on the field more times than he was standing. The same would hold true for Leaf, as he would join a Chargers team that had gone 4-12, and while they were a little better than the Colts, they ended the season on an eight-game losing streak.

Rookie Seasonxix

Peyton was the Colts' starting quarterback from his very first practice. The Colts knew that there was no one else to consider. The first couple of games were rough for the young Manning, as he threw three interceptions during the season-opening loss to the Miami Dolphins, 24-15, on September 6, 1998. It was a daunting game for the rookie considering he was going up against legendary quarterback Dan Marino. Manning did have some bright spots in the match. His first completion of the game was to running back Marshall Faulk, who would become a Hall-of-Fame caliber player, for 15 yards. That opening drive reached Miami territory before running back Zack Crockett fumbled the ball to the Dolphins.

Manning recovered with a 42-yard pass to Marvin Harrison on the very next drive, and the two often connected – the start of a fantastic duo in Indianapolis. Despite the three interceptions against Miami, he completed 21 of 37 for 302 yards and a 6-yard touchdown to Harrison, who finished with 102 yards on five catches.

Manning lost the first four games of the season and had only three touchdown passes in that span while throwing 11 interceptions. The Colts got their first win of the season against the San Diego Chargers, providing fans with their first look at Manning versus Leaf, the top two picks in the 1998 NFL Draft. Manning struck first with a 19-yard touchdown pass to Faulk in the first quarter, followed by a two-point conversion run by Ken Dilger for the early lead. The only other touchdown came from San Diego's Natrone Means, but Indianapolis won the game thanks to Mike Vanderjagt's field goals from 48, 51, and 40 yards for a final score of 17-12. Leaf struggled, completing 12 of 23 for 160 yards and one interception. Manning also went 12 of 23 for 137 yards, the touchdown pass to Faulk, and one interception.

While Peyton had a great rookie year concerning statistics, he was also reportedly depressed over his performance. He was mainly dissatisfied with the fact that he threw a league-high 28 interceptions. That was also the most interceptions he ever threw in an NFL season. He was still putting up some good numbers, but there were some close games that the Colts lost where maybe an interception was a factor in keeping points off the board. Ten of Indianapolis' 13 losses his rookie season were by single digits. But adjusting to the professional ranks can take some time, and the numbers did get better in the second half of the season despite Manning throwing two or more interceptions in 11 games.

There are many opinions as to why Peyton threw so many interceptions in his rookie year. However, most analysts believe it was because of his competitiveness. He wanted his team to drive the ball down the field and score touchdowns every single time. He wanted to a make big plays every down. In short, many believe that his extreme competitiveness was also impatience, and that is what drove him toward having so many interceptions. Others think Peyton just never realized how good the defensive lines are in the NFL, and he underrated their abilities. Peyton realized that the NFL was a different playing field for him, a faster one than college, and he was going to have to take his skills as a leading quarterback to a whole new level.

However, despite the fact that Peyton felt he had a rough rookie year, the coaching staff in Indianapolis told him not to worry about it and that, no matter what, he was still going to be their starting quarterback. That meant Peyton had to shrug off the disappointment and move forward. Even with those 28 interceptions in his rookie season in the NFL, Manning never realized that he was to become the greatest quarterback.

He also did not notice that the rest of his statistics were far better than many football experts would have believed possible when predicting how he would do in his first NFL season. In fact, Peyton ended up breaking five NFL records as a rookie. One of these records was most touchdown passes in a single season with 26. Peyton was also named to the NFL All-Rookie First Team of 1998. He threw for 3,739 yards, barely missing the 4000–yard mark, something that is extremely hard for even an experienced NFL quarterback to accomplish in that era of the NFL.

The Colts ended the season with a terrible 3-13 record. Incidentally, this was the same record they had the previous year. Besides a 6-10 mark in 2001, this was the only other season in which Peyton would end up with a losing record. In fact, in just his second season, he would completely flip the record around, with 13 wins and only three losses. The good news was that things were going to be looking up from here.

1999 Season[xx]

Without a doubt, the 1999 season was the year when Peyton solidified his position as the starting quarterback in Indianapolis. After a disastrous rookie year season, Peyton helped the Colts to one of the greatest single-season turnarounds in NFL history while cutting his interceptions nearly in half.

During the first game on September 12, the Colts clobbered the Buffalo Bills by a score of 31-14. Manning went 21 of 33 for 284 yards, with two touchdown passes to Harrison, but the negative was that he also had two interceptions. Manning added another three touchdowns, all to Harrison, but also was picked off twice in a 31-28 loss to the New England Patriots on September 19. However, the Colts bounced back with a win over Leaf and the San Diego Chargers on September 26 by a score of 27-19. Despite a ball being snapped out of the end zone to give San Diego a two-point safety and throwing another interception, Peyton threw for 404 yards and two touchdowns – a 33-yard pass to Harrison and a 26-yarder to Terrence Wilkins – to give him his first AFC Offensive Player of the Week honors.

After a tough 34-31 loss at home to the Miami Dolphins in which the Colts blew a nine-point fourth-quarter lead, Peyton and the Indianapolis Colts won their next 11 games in their push to the top of the AFC playoff standings. During this time, Manning completed 62.8

percent of his passes with 16 touchdowns to only nine interceptions. He also ran for a 7-yard touchdown run in the fourth quarter for the go-ahead score in a 25-17 win over the Kansas City Chiefs on November 17. His best game statistically of the season was a 44-17 win on the road against the Philadelphia Eagles on November 21, when Manning completed 16 passes for 235 yards and three touchdowns, including an 80-yarder to Wilkins in the third quarter and a 17-yard pass to running back Edgerrin James to make the game 44-3.

In all, they ended the season with a record of 13-3, winning the AFC East and claiming the number 2 seed in the playoffs behind Jacksonville. From the previous year, they had completely inverted their game record. They accomplished something that many fans and critics would have never thought possible this quickly after the disappointment of 1997. Peyton did not just confirm that he had the qualities of a championship-contending player and that he could lead his team to victory, but he also gave the Colts another promise: as long as Peyton remained as their quarterback, a Super Bowl win would be almost inevitable.

Who could argue against Peyton ended after he finished the regular season with 4,135 passing yards, 26 touchdowns, and 15 interceptions? The numbers proved his ability to lead his team to victory. Peyton was named second-team All-Pro and went to the Pro Bowl in 2000. The Colts looked strong as the second seed in the AFC and had a first-round bye before playing the Tennessee Titans on

January 16, 2000 – a week after the Titans came up with the Music City Miracle play to defeat the Buffalo Bills in the wildcard round.

Tennessee continued to be a team of destiny as the Titans defeated the Colts 19-16. Manning tried to engineer a late rally and scored on a 15-yard touchdown run with less than two minutes left to bring the game to within a field goal, but the Titans recovered Mike Vanderjagt's ensuing onside kick. Outside of that, Manning was not very effective against the Titans' defense as he went 19 of 42 for 227 yards in his postseason debut.

However, the fact that Peyton was able to make it to the playoffs in only his second season as starting quarterback gave the Colts hope, something that they had been missing all this time. The Colts now realized they were a playoff-caliber team in the NFL so long as Peyton Manning was their quarterback.

2000 Season[xxi]

The Colts got 2000 off to a great start with a 27-14 win over the Kansas City Chiefs on September 3, where Peyton threw for 273 yards. But this was quickly followed up with a 38-31 loss at home to the Oakland Raiders. He completed 33 of 38 passes for 367 yards and three touchdowns, but his two interceptions were costly. Inconsistency continued with Peyton showing a mixture of good and bad games, and the Colts would finish with a record of 10-6.

30

There were games like the one the Colts played against the New England Patriots on October 22, 2000, when Peyton achieved a perfect 158.3 passer rating for the first time in his NFL career during a 30-23 win. He completed 16 of 20 for 268 yards and three touchdowns. It was a much different game than the first game against the Patriots two weeks prior in Foxboro, Massachusetts, where Manning had to throw 54 times in a 24-16 loss. He did complete 31 passes for 334 yards and one touchdown, but he was also intercepted three times. There were games in which Manning threw for more than 300 yards and games in which he failed to break 200. The team looked strong in the season finale against the Minnesota Vikings on December 24, when Manning went 25 of 36 for 283 yards with four touchdown passes, including three to his favorite target Harrison, while the other was a 52-yard scoring toss to James.

With their 10-6 record and runner-up finish in the AFC East, the Colts claimed the second wild-card spot and were the sixth seed in the playoffs. Manning would again fail to notch his first playoff victory as Indianapolis fell to divisional rival Miami 23-17 in overtime in the wild-card round.

The Colts held the lead late in the game after Manning completed a 17-yard pass to Jerome Pathon in the second quarter and got a 50-yard field goal from Mike Vanderjagt for a 17-10 lead with 4:55 to play in regulation. But Jay Fielder led the Dolphins on a late touchdown drive, tying the game with 34 seconds remaining to force sudden death. Manning put the Colts in position to win, but Vanderjagt missed a 49-

yard field goal and the Dolphins took the ensuing possession 61 yards, capped by Lamar Smith's 17-yard touchdown run, to the end zone for the win.

2001 Season[xxii]

The 2001 season was the year the Colts introduced their no-huddle offense, which quickly became the signature method Manning used to drive the football downfield, and fans started seeing a quarterback who made adjustments at the line with shouts like "Omaha." The change in the team's offensive game plan worked out well in the first two games of the regular season. They defeated the Jets in New York, 45-24, on September 9, and the Buffalo Bills at home 42-26 two weeks later. Manning had 421 yards and four touchdowns while completing 23 of 29 passes against the Bills.

The momentum died quickly after the Colts were blown out 44-13 at New England in what would be the first of many clashes with Patriots quarterback Tom Brady. He threw for only 168 yards but did not throw any interceptions. Manning was picked off three times, and Otis Smith and Ty Law returned theirs for touchdowns.

It was the first of three straight losses. But the struggles for the Colts truly began on November 11, when a 27-24 home loss to the Miami Dolphins started a run of seven losses in eight games down the stretch. Manning had interception problems that reminded fans of his rookie season. In 2001, Manning threw 23 interceptions, a negative mark on what otherwise was a decent year with 4,131 yards and 26

32

touchdowns, along with completing 62.7 percent of his throws. Manning also had success running the ball with four rushing touchdowns and an average of nearly 4.5 yards per carry. Still, the Colts stumbled to a 6-10 mark and a fourth-place finish in the AFC East.

Fans were not happy, but the blame was not solely on Manning. The defense had struggles of its own as the Colts gave up a league-worst 486 points, which averages out to more than 30 per game. For this and other reasons, management in Indianapolis decided to make a coaching change at the end of the season from Jim Mora to the defensive-minded Tony Dungy.

2002 Season[xxiii]

While the 2001 season was crucial for Peyton's improvement because it was the beginning of him utilizing his signature no-huddle offense, 2002 marked another turning point for Peyton as Dungy took over. It was the start of a seven-year run after Dungy had been the coach for the Tampa Bay Buccaneers for six seasons. Dungy had reached the playoffs four times with the Buccaneers and reached the 1999 NFC title game, but had never gotten to the Super Bowl. He was eventually fired because owner Malcolm Glazer considered Dungy too conservative of a play-caller offensively.

There were some growing pains during the season, as any team would have with a new head coach, especially one not used to having a franchise quarterback who could do just about anything asked of him offensively. It also marked the first season following the radical realignment in which the Houston Texans entered the league as the NFL's 32nd team. The league then moved Seattle back to the NFC to create two balanced 16-team conferences in which there would be four four-team divisions. The Colts were placed in the AFC South with the expansion Texans, Tennessee Titans, and Jacksonville Jaguars, all new division opponents after being part of the AFC East since the 1970 AFL-NFL merger while the team was located in Baltimore.

Indianapolis won four of their first five games. It started with three touchdowns and 211 yards for Manning in the team's 28-25 season-opening win over Jacksonville on September 8. Manning had a near-perfect game and completed 21 of 28 passes two weeks later during a 23-3 win over the expansion Houston Texans. But the Colts hit a roadblock in their offensive progression with three straight losses, during which Manning was picked off six times against the Pittsburgh Steelers, Washington Redskins, and Tennessee Titans. Manning and the Colts still fought for a playoff spot thanks to a 35-13 win over the Philadelphia Eagles on November 10, a game in which Manning threw for 319 yards and three touchdowns. That was followed by a 20-3 win over Dallas the next week where Manning was a skillful 29 of 38 for 252 yards and two TD passes.

At the end of the regular season, the Colts were 10-6 and finished second in the AFC South, which was good enough to earn a wildcard playoff spot. But the momentum of going 6-2 in the second half of the season behind a quarterback who accumulated 4,200 yards and 27 touchdowns – disappeared in the playoffs. Manning suffered the worst playoff loss of his career to that point on January 4, 2003.

Manning fell to 0-3 in the postseason in a humbling 41-0 road rout administered by the New York Jets, who limited him to 14 of 31 passing for 137 yards and two interceptions. His counterpart Chad Pennington looked more the Pro Bowl-caliber quarterback with a 56-yard scoring pass to Richie Anderson on New York's first possession, and it snowballed from there. It was the second-worst shutout loss in NFL playoff history, behind only Chicago's 73-0 thrashing of Washington in the 1940 NFL title game.

"I tried to be patient," Manning told The Associated Press after the game. "But I got to be impatient because the more you get in the hole, the more they take you out of your game plan. So I ended up doing a lot of things I shouldn't have."

2003 Season[xxiv]

The bitter taste of that loss provided Manning plenty of additional motivation. That is because 2003 saw some improvements for Manning and the rest of the team that led to the first postseason victory of his career. The Colts were undefeated in their first five games with Manning more efficient in the passing game. However, no one expected what happened during their game in New Orleans on September 28: a 55-21 win in Manning's third perfect QB rating performance. Manning had a 17-yard TD pass to Ricky Williams

35

before hooking up with Harrison on scoring plays of 14 and 79 yards to stake Indianapolis to a 21-0 lead. Overall, Manning completed 21 of 27 for 327 yards with six touchdowns – which is why he was named the Player of the Week in the NFL. It would not be the only time Manning surprised fans in 2003.

On October 6 while visiting the Buccaneers and Dungy's old stomping grounds in Tampa Bay for the first time since arriving in Indianapolis, the Colts were trailing 35-14 with less than five minutes remaining. After James Mungro's 3-yard touchdown run with 3:37 left, the Colts recovered an onside kick to set up a 28-yard pass from Manning to Harrison. Indianapolis recovered a second consecutive onside kick to get the ball back with 1:41 remaining in the game. Manning led the quick drive that ended with Williams punching it in from 1 yard to tie the game. The game went into overtime where Vanderjagt nailed a 29-yard field goal for the 38-35 win – giving the Colts the NFL record for the biggest comeback victory with less than four minutes left in regulation and giving fans hope that their team was the team of destiny.

And as the Colts continued winning, Manning continued to improve down the stretch, including a five-touchdown performance in a 38-7 win over the Atlanta Falcons on December 14. The Colts finished 12-4 and won their first AFC South title. But the Colts were only able to get the third seed in the conference because New England finished 14-2, followed by Kansas City at 13-3. Manning's regular-season success concerning statistics carried over for the first time in his NFL career.

But the division title carried home-field advantage, and this time, Manning and Colts used it to full effect in the wildcard round. Manning looked nearly flawless in a 41-10 win over the Denver Broncos on January 4, 2004. In his first career playoff victory, Manning completed 22 of 26 passes for 377 yards and five touchdowns. Three of the scoring plays exceeded 30 yards, including an 87-yarder to Brandon Stokley in the closing moments of the first half that made it 28-3. The only negative was a fumble on his only recorded rushing attempt.

One week later in the AFC Divisional Playoffs, Manning completed 73.3 percent of his throws for 304 yards and three touchdowns in a 38-31 road win at Kansas City. In his first two playoff wins, Manning was 44 of 56 for 681 yards and eight TDs without an interception as the Colts reached the conference title game for the first time since 1995.

But in his way was what would become all-too familiar arch-nemeses in Brady, head coach Bill Belichick, and the New England Patriots. A defensive mastermind, Belichick has befuddled many an opposing quarterback with his various schemes and unconventional personnel deployment. He is one of the masters of "exotic packages" in which formations and coverage are well-disguised until right before the ball is snapped. The game within the game of Manning trying to solve Belichick's defenses on every snap would rage for well over a decade as the two vied for AFC supremacy.

And in this first playoff clash, it was all Belichick and the Patriots as they intercepted Manning four times in a 24-14 win over the Colts. Manning completed 23 of 47 passes for 237 yards and a touchdown, but Indianapolis was unable to overcome five total turnovers while New England was able to settle for field goals on drives that stalled.

While the Colts and Peyton Manning were unsuccessful in making it to the Super Bowl, they made progress in reaching the AFC title game for the first time in eight years. These advances would eventually result in reaching the Super Bowl in future seasons. While Peyton Manning would often receive multiple awards throughout the season, he won the ESPY Award for the Best NFL Player (Most Valuable Player) for the first time. This is considered one of the most prestigious awards to be received by a professional NFL player. In the 2003 season, Peyton had a league-leading 4,267 yards along with 29 touchdowns. The Colts' passing game had become a formidable weapon with playmakers Harrison, James, Stokley, and Reggie Wayne.

2004 Season[xxv]

The 2004 season was one in which Peyton returned to the playoffs while also continuing to set records once thought unachievable. After suffering a tough 27-24 loss to New England to open the season September 9, Manning caught fire and led the Colts to another AFC South championship with a 12-4 record. In Week 3 on September 26 against the Green Bay Packers, Manning connected on 28 of 40

38

passes for 393 yards and five touchdowns in a 45-31 shootout victory over Brett Favre, who had 360 yards and four touchdown passes himself.

As the season progressed, fans reading the box scores took notice of the statistics Manning was compiling as he had six games of four or more touchdown passes in the first 11. But he took it to another level on Thanksgiving at Detroit on November 25, shredding the Lions secondary by going 23 of 28 for 236 yards and six TD passes in a 41-9 romp. It was on the few times backup quarterback Jim Sorgi saw playing time, and James rushed for 105 yards.

The Colts won eight of their last nine games and led the league in scoring with 422 points. Manning eclipsed Marino's single-season touchdown NFL record with 49 touchdown passes in just 15 games. He was also third in the league with 4,557 yards, which set a career high. Despite the regular-season success, Indianapolis was once again relegated to the number 3 seed as Pittsburgh went 15-1 and New England followed close behind at 14-2.

Manning barely played in Week 17 at Denver, with Dungy opting to rest most of his starters since the Colts were already locked in as the number 3 seed. Whether refreshed or otherwise, Manning looked exceptional in ripping the Broncos for 458 yards and four touchdown passes in a 49-24 victory at home.

But the divisional round meant another trip to New England, and the Patriots again stifled Manning as they advanced to the AFC title game by handing the Colts a 20-3 loss. The game was a defensive battle for the first two-plus quarters with the Patriots holding a 6-3 lead. Indianapolis opted to punt on a 4th-and-1 from the New England 49, and the Patriots marched 87 yards on 15 plays on a touchdown drive that spanned more than eight minutes to make it 13-3. After New England's defense stiffened once more early in the fourth quarter, Brady killed off the game with a 14-play, 94-yard drive he capped with a one-yard plunge for the final margin with 7:10 to play.

Manning finished a respectable 27 for 42 for 238 yards, but he failed to throw a touchdown pass and was intercepted once. But he was not the sole reason the Colts failed to advance as their run defense was gashed for 210 yards by the Patriots as they held the ball for more than 37 minutes. Sometimes the best way to defeat Peyton Manning is to keep him off the field.

2005 Season[xxvi]

Dungy and the Colts revamped their defense to go along with the high-powered offense led by Manning as defensive ends Robert Mathis and Dwight Freeney formed an imposing pass-rush combination while linebacker Cato June plugged things up in the middle. After giving up 351 points in 2004, the Colts shaved more than 100 points off that total in 2005, yielding just 247, or 15.4 per game for the NFL's second-best scoring defense.

Offensively, James became more of a focal point as the offense gained better balance. And with the two sides in harmony, Manning and the Colts put together one of the best seasons in franchise history. The defense set the tone with a 5-0 start in which the Colts allowed just two touchdowns and 29 points in wins over Jacksonville, Baltimore, Cleveland, Tennessee, and San Francisco. Manning was steady over that span, with his best game coming in a 31-10 rout of the Titans in which he completed 20 of 27 passes for 264 yards and four touchdowns.

Manning did not have to save the day until Indianapolis faced St. Louis in Week 6, when he rallied the Colts from an early 17-7 deficit to record a 45-28 victory. But even in that win, the defense helped out by forcing two turnovers deep in Rams territory that fueled a 21-point fourth-quarter.

Manning then found his groove over the next three games, throwing for 855 yards and three touchdowns. The most significant victory in that span was the middle game at New England where Peyton defeated the Patriots for the first time in eight games with a 40-21 victory at Foxborough. Manning finished 28 of 37 for 321 yards and three touchdowns, and as he watched Brady kill off last season's playoff game, he forced his New England counterpart to stand helplessly on the sidelines as he marched the Colts down the field for a game-sealing touchdown in the fourth quarter.

Indianapolis improved to 10-0 by surviving a 45-37 shootout at Cincinnati, where Manning and Carson Palmer combined to throw for 700 yards and five touchdowns. The defense returned to form in the next two games, wins over Pittsburgh and Tennessee, limiting them to 10 points while Manning efficiently carved up those defenses for five touchdown passes.

At 12-0, there was talk of Indianapolis being able to run the table and join the 1972 Miami Dolphins as the only teams to go unbeaten in the regular season. The Colts made it 13 for 13 the following week by holding on for a 26-18 victory at Jacksonville as Manning threw for 336 yards and a touchdown.

The Colts had already wrapped up their third straight AFC South title and home-field advantage throughout the playoffs. Now they were playing for a shot at history. Into Indianapolis came the San Diego Chargers, who were fighting for their playoff lives at 8-5 and tied for second in the AFC West.

After not trailing in more than eight games dating back to mid-October, Manning and the Colts found themselves on the wrong end of a 16-0 scoreline with 9:30 left in the third quarter. Indianapolis did not get a first down until the second quarter, and San Diego made a goal-line stand on 4th-and-1 to preserve a 7-0 lead. But Manning rallied the Colts as they reeled off 17 consecutive points in a 6:01 span to take a one-point lead late in the third quarter.

The Chargers, though, had a competent signal-caller of their own in Drew Brees, and he did not back down. He guided San Diego to a go-ahead field goal with the key play a 54-yard pass to Nate Kaeding. The Chargers then added a backbreaking touchdown on an 83-yard run by Michael Turner with 2:09 left to make it 26-17, and there would be no late rally this time as the Colts lost for the first time in 2005.

Manning finished with 336 yards and a touchdown, but he was picked off twice and harassed all day. San Diego recorded four sacks, a high total considering that Indianapolis had yielded just 11 in the first 13 games, and its 3-4 defense was able to force Peyton out of the pocket where he is less comfortable.

With nothing to play for, not much was made of Indianapolis dropping a second straight game at Seattle despite it being labeled as a potential Super Bowl preview. Manning barely played in the season finale against Arizona as Sorgi guided the Colts to a 17-13 win. The Colts finished a franchise-best 14-2, and the road to Super Bowl 40 would go through Indianapolis and the RCA Dome.

It was another season of statistical superlatives for Manning, who became the first quarterback to throw for at least 3,000 yards in each of his first eight seasons. He and Harrison also set an NFL record for the most touchdown passes between a quarterback and receiver, bettering the mark of 86 established by Hall of Famers Steve Young and Jerry Rice of the San Francisco 49ers.

If the playoffs held true to form, the Colts would have faced the Patriots in the divisional round after the AFC East champs beat Jacksonville 28-3 in the wild-card round. But the sixth-seeded Steelers upset AFC North rival Cincinnati, sending New England to

Denver and earning a trip to the Midwest. And the day before the Colts played, they watched the Broncos dispose of the Patriots. But unlike the Colts' 26-7 win at home over Pittsburgh on Monday Night Football to cap Week 12, the Steelers showed plenty of playoff mettle. They took the opening kickoff 84 yards for a touchdown and shook off an early interception by Ben Roethlisberger, who made it 14-0 with a 7-yard touchdown pass to Heath Miller with 3:12 left in the opening quarter.

Pittsburgh would eventually extend their lead to 21-3 late in the third quarter before Manning and the Colts would rally. First, it was a 50-yard scoring pass to Dallas Clark to make it 21-10 with 14:09 to play. After the Steelers chewed up more than eight minutes on their ensuing drive, Manning directed a devastating no-huddle offense as the Colts went 80 yards on six plays in just 99 seconds as James bulled in from three yards with 4:24 left. Manning found Wayne for the two-point conversion, and it was 21-18 with everything to play for.

It looked dire for the Colts after Manning was sacked on a 4th-and-16 that gave Pittsburgh the ball at the Indianapolis 2-yard line with 1:20 to play. On the next play, Steelers running back Jerome Bettis tried to score a game-sealing touchdown but fumbled after a hit by linebacker Gary Brackett. Safety Nick Harper picked up the ball and raced in the opposite direction with what would have been one of the most miraculous postseason touchdowns in NFL history.

Except Roethlisberger, who saw the disaster unfurl after the handoff, began to run as Harper tried to break away from the chasing pack. He tried to juke Roethlisberger and almost succeeded, but the Steelers quarterback was able to trip up Harper near midfield. Still, Peyton and the Colts had some life with 1:09 to go, and they did not even need a touchdown. They just needed a field goal to force overtime.

Manning first hit Wayne with a 22-yard pass to get into Steelers territory and then found Harrison for an eight-yard gain to the Pittsburgh 28. After a timeout, Manning was incomplete on two attempts to find Wayne, trying to win the game on the first one with a shot in the end zone and set up a 46-yard attempt for Vanderjagt, who had now become the most accurate field goal kicker in NFL history at 87.5 percent. But it was not to be for Manning as the kick from the left hash mark sailed well wide of the right goalpost.

A season that had the look of greatness was now trashed, and the whispers about whether Manning and the Colts would ever get to a Super Bowl, let alone win one, were now openly spoken questions. They were the first team to go 11-0 and not reach the Super Bowl in NFL history. The fact that Manning had been well under wraps by the Steelers aggressive defense left a bitter taste in the quarterback's mouth as he tried to process the defeat.

"There is no question we were in a good position with home field and having the bye," he told USA Today. "I'm disappointed. It will be more disappointing tonight and tomorrow, and it certainly takes time to move on from a game like this."

He also knew how empty his legacy would be, even at that point in his career, without lifting the Vince Lombardi trophy, admitting he could not counter the critics who said that he would never be among the game's best without a Super Bowl win. But Peyton also stated that "I'm going to keep trying."

Manning was denied a third straight NFL Most Valuable Player award as he finished runner-up to Seattle Seahawks running back Shaun Alexander, whose team was unable to overcome the Steelers in Super Bowl 40. Manning finished with 3,747 yards, which would turn out to be his lowest total over a full season for the rest of his career. But there was still plenty of unfinished business for Peyton and the Colts.

2006 Season[xxvii]

Fans had begun to draw parallels between Manning and Marino, another quarterback who put up breathtaking numbers but failed to win a Super Bowl title. For all of Marino's prowess, since he retired owning almost all of the league's most important passing records, his only Super Bowl appearance came in 1985 after his second season with the Miami Dolphins.

But 2006 would be the season that completely changed the era for Peyton Manning and the Colts. It started on September 10 against the

New York Giants in which Peyton would face his younger brother Eli, who was now well entrenched in his third season. This was the first time that two quarterbacks who were brothers faced each other in the NFL, and they took a photo to commemorate the occasion. Eli had more touchdown passes, but Peyton emerged with the victory as he threw for 276 yards and a score in the 26-21 road win.

Manning led the Colts to a 9-0 start as he won AFC Offensive Player of the Week honors twice. In a 43-24 win against the Texans, Manning threw for 400 yards and three touchdowns, with newcomers Joseph Addai and Bryan Fletcher on the receiving end for two of them. Manning looked unstoppable during a 36-22 win on October 22 over the Washington Redskins, in which he had a 51-yard pass to Reggie Wayne as one of his four scoring tosses to go with 342 yards. He followed that up by going 32 of 39 for 345 yards and three touchdowns in a 34-31 win against Denver, capping that game by going 5-for-5 for 47 yards on the game's final drive. This set up a game-winning 37-yard field goal by Adam Vinatieri, who arrived from New England in the offseason after Vanderjagt was released.

Manning again got the best of Brady in a 27-20 win at New England, throwing for 326 yards and a pair of TD passes as Indianapolis improved to 8-0. The unbeaten season would end two weeks later with a 21-14 setback at Dallas on November 19, starting a curious run of inconsistency in which Indianapolis looked like world-beaters at home and anything but on the road. In the three victories at the RCA Dome while helping the Colts to their fourth straight AFC South title,

Manning completed just under 70 percent of his passes for 747 yards and seven touchdowns with only one interception. In the four road losses, he completed 60.4 percent of his passes for 1,123 yards and six touchdowns with five interceptions.

With a 12-4 finish, the Colts were the number 3 seed in the AFC behind San Diego and Baltimore. They opened the postseason against Kansas City in the wild-card round and emerged with a gritty 23-8 victory over the Chiefs. Manning did a lot of things right, like completing 30 of 38 passes, but he was also picked off three times and did not put away the game until hooking up with Wayne on an 8-yard touchdown pass in the fourth quarter for the game's final points.

That learned perseverance would come in handy in the divisional round at Baltimore. The Ravens had put together a defense for the ages and allowed a league-low 201 points. They also had 28 interceptions as safeties Ed Reed and Dawan Landry had five apiece while cornerback Chris McAlister had a team-high six. And they also had the game's best linebacking tandem in Ray Lewis and Bart Scott.

And while the Colts had played in Baltimore, the city they left in 1984 well before Manning would become the famous player he was, on three previous occasions, this was the first playoff game between the teams since Irsay's famous stealth move in the dead of night to go 600 miles west. Some Baltimore fans still held a grudge almost 23 years later.

Even Manning noted the atmosphere, telling USA Today that there were "a lot of middle fingers on the bus ride coming in."

Every yard was fiercely contested, and both defenses rose to the occasion as neither team breached the other's end zone. Instead, the game hinged on Vinatieri, who is known as the most clutch NFL kickers in history. He earned every bit of his five-year, $12 million contract on that day in Baltimore as Manning put the Colts in position to score before Vinatieri delivered five times in as many attempts.

Manning completed just 15 of 30 attempts and was picked off twice and sacked once while throwing for 170 yards. But he also did just enough to keep the chains moving by converting 8 of 19 third-down plays before Vinatieri booted field goals of 23, 42, 51, 48 and 35 yards to power Indianapolis to a 15-6 victory and a spot in the AFC title game.

The AFC title game would pit the Colts against Brady and the Patriots, though this time it would be in Indianapolis. At the outset, though, it looked like home-field advantage was anything but as New England stormed to a 21-3 lead after Asante Samuel picked off Manning and raced 39 yards for a touchdown in the second quarter.

While it did not look like much at the time, the Colts settled down despite settling for a field goal right before halftime. Vinatieri drilled a 26-yarder with seven seconds left to cap a 15-play, 80-yard drive that left a 21-6 deficit after two quarters. More importantly, Manning would start the second half on offense with a chance to build on that momentum.

And he did just that to start the third quarter, directing a 76-yard drive that drew Indianapolis within 21-13 after a quarterback sneak over the goal line. On the next possession, Manning again marched the Colts 76 yards, this time using a little bit of trickery as he floated a touchdown pass to defensive tackle Dan Klecko. The two-point conversion pass to Harrison knotted the game at 21 with four minutes left in the third quarter and turned it into a slugfest between Manning and Brady. The man with the ball in his hands last was likely going to be the victor.

Befitting his status as one of the game's greats, Brady quickly put the Patriots back on top with a touchdown pass of his own. Manning responded with another scoring drive, but this one ended with a little bit of luck for the Colts as center Jeff Saturday recovered a fumble by running back Dominic Rhodes in the end zone to forge a 28-all tie with 13:24 left.

Vinatieri's successor, Stephen Gostkowski, booted field goals of 28 and 43 yards around a 36-yarder by Vinatieri to give New England a 34-31 lead with 3:49 to play. Manning, though, was unable to move the ball and Indianapolis was forced to punt the ball back to New England after three incompletions. This was the bleakest situation Manning had been in over his career, to come so close to a Super Bowl appearance but watching it slip away from the sideline.

The Colts' defense, though, rallied to the occasion and forced a three-and-out of their own. They gave Peyton the ball back at his 20-yard line with 2:17 to play and two timeouts. Eighty yards is an eternity of time for a quarterback who was the master of a no-huddle offense.

First, he hit Wayne for an 11-yard gain. After an incompletion, he hooked up with Fletcher for a 32-yard pass to the New England 37. Manning was able to squeeze in one more play before the two-minute warning, and it was a crucial one as he found Wayne for 14 yards, and a roughing the passer penalty on New England advanced the ball to the Patriots' 11.

The Colts were safely in field goal range, but now Manning had a chance to win. Two rushes by Addai netted eight yards, and the Patriots called a timeout in hopes they could give Brady one last chance. And in a wry twist of irony, Manning handed off to Addai one more time for the go-ahead points after throwing a total of 292 touchdown passes in the regular season and playoffs up to that point in his career.

But there was still one minute left, and as everyone knows, you can never count out Brady. Two completions moved New England to the Indianapolis 45 as the seconds ticked down in agonizingly slow fashion, to the point Manning could not bear to watch the action unfold from the sidelines. But the raucous cheers inside the RCA Dome after Marlin Jackson intercepted Brady told him everything he needed to know.

Peyton Manning was finally going to the Super Bowl for the first time in his nine-year career after an exhausting 38-34 win over his arch-rivals that marked the largest deficit overcome in a conference title game in NFL history.

"I don't get into monkeys or vindication. I don't play that card," he told The Associated Press. "I know how hard I worked this season; I know how hard I worked this week.

"I said a little prayer on that last drive. I don't know if you're supposed to pray for stuff like that, but I said a little prayer."

The Colts would play the Chicago Bears in Super Bowl 41 in Miami, with the "Monsters of the Midway" making their first Super Bowl appearance since winning the 1985 title behind one of the best defenses in league history. This edition of Chicago's defense was no slouch either; the Bears went 13-3 and yielded a conference-low 255 points. While they did not have the offensive weapons that Manning and the Colts had, they had the NFL's best special teams player in cornerback Devin Hester, who had an astonishing six touchdowns via punt returns, kickoff returns, and a missed field goal return.

Still, the Colts were prohibitive betting favorites to win the Super Bowl and were favored by nearly a touchdown to win by Las Vegas oddsmakers by the time kickoff rolled around.

The game could not have started any worse for the Colts as Hester took the opening kickoff 92 yards for a touchdown to give the Bears a

7-0 lead just 14 seconds into the game. Peyton and the offense had the jitters early as he misfired on his first two passes while the offensive line took two penalties. Indianapolis' first possession ended when Manning was picked off on a deep fly pattern by Chris Harris near midfield.

Peyton fared far better the next time he had the ball, mixing in run plays with Addai against a defense that played its safeties deep and was willing to concede short passing plays while denying Harrison and Wayne to get free deep. Manning exposed Chicago's "Cover-2" scheme by stepping up into the pocket and finding a wide-open Wayne behind the defense for a 53-yard touchdown pass to make it 7-6.

The Colts recovered a fumble on the ensuing kickoff, but the slick conditions created by a steady rain helped neither team as Manning fumbled the ball right back to the Bears on the next play. Chicago took full advantage and extended their lead to 14-6. Vinatieri drew Indianapolis within 14-9 on a 29-yard field goal before Manning engineered a 58-yard drive that Rhodes capped by bulling his way in from one yard with 6:09 to go in the first half.

Indianapolis would never trail again once Vinatieri booted a pair of third-quarter field goals to extend the lead to 22-14. The Bears would close within five points, but Kelvin Hayden would seal the Colts' first Super Bowl title in 36 years by returning an interception 54 yards in the fourth quarter to cap a 29-17 victory. Manning had solid numbers, completing 25 of 38 passes for 247 yards to win MVP honors, but it was also a team effort. Rhodes and Addai combined for 190 rushing yards while the defense forced five turnovers.

"In the past when our team's come up short, it's been disappointing," Manning told ESPN. "Somehow, we found a way to have learned from those bad losses, and we've been a better team because of it. As disappointing as the playoff loss was last year to Pittsburgh, the veteran guys got together and learned from it and felt we were a better team this year and maybe stronger for it.

"It's nice when you put a lot of hard work to cap it off with a championship."[xxviii]

2007 Season[xxix]

There would be few signs of a Super Bowl hangover in 2007 as Manning and the Colts burst from the gates by winning their first seven games. He threw for 1,833 yards and 13 touchdowns with only three interceptions in that run, highlighted by three-touchdown games against New Orleans and Denver. Indianapolis had a midseason hiccup with close losses to New England and San Diego by a combined six points with Manning throwing a career-worst six interceptions in a 23-21 loss to the Chargers, but the Colts would regroup to win their next six games as they wrapped up a fifth straight AFC South title with ease.

With nothing to play for in the season finale having wrapped up the number 2 seed in the AFC, Manning gave way to Sorgi in Indianapolis' season-ending 16-10 loss to Tennessee. The Colts would be the number 2 seed, but the talk of the NFL that season was the Patriots, who became just the second team in league history to go unbeaten in the regular season and the first to go 16-0.

Manning, though, would never get a crack at that Patriots team in the postseason. Despite throwing for 402 yards and three touchdowns, the Colts fell at home 28-24 to the San Diego Chargers as backup quarterback Billy Volek filled in for the injured Philip Rivers and rallied San Diego late. Manning, who also was picked off twice, nearly pulled out a victory from the jaws of defeat, but his 4th-and-goal pass to Addai from the Chargers' 7-yard line fell incomplete. Manning finished with 4,040 passing yards and 31 touchdowns, but falling short of repeating as Super Bowl champions left the quarterback far from satisfied.

"What happened last year doesn't make it any easier," he told The AP. "When you come back and commit yourself to the '07 season, and you don't finish it like you want to, it hurts."

2008 Season[xxx]

Manning played the entire regular season despite missing training camp and the pre-season due to a knee injury. But the rust from missing most of the preseason was evident as the Colts dropped two of their first three games and were 3-4 after a 31-21 loss at Tennessee in Week 8.

The season turned around the following week with an 18-15 win over archrival New England. Manning threw for 254 yards and two touchdowns and led the Colts on a 48-yard drive for the go-ahead points on Vinatieri's 52-yard field goal with 8:05 to play.

That would spark a nine-game winning streak that would carry the Colts into the playoffs, but this time as the wildcard as their 12-4 mark was second to the Titans' 13-3 record. The "reward" for having the best wildcard record was playing the worst division winner, and it also served up a chance for revenge as the Colts would travel west to face San Diego. The Chargers finished the season 8-8 but won their last four games to overtake the Broncos for the AFC West title, and more importantly, home-field advantage for this match.

It was a back-and-forth contest, with the Colts scoring first on a 1-yard plunge by Addai. San Diego regrouped to take a 14-10 halftime lead, but Manning and Wayne hooked up for a 72-yard scoring play to give Indianapolis back the lead in the third quarter. The score remained 17-14 until Nate Kaeding made a 26-yard field goal with 31 seconds left in regulation to tie the game.

Manning, who finished 25 of 42 for 310 yards and a touchdown, never stepped on the field in overtime as the Chargers won the coin toss and eventually the game as Darren Sproles rushed 22 yards to paydirt to deal the Colts a 23-17 setback.

Concerning statistics, Manning had another solid year with 4,002 passing yards and 27 touchdowns, but the lack of a consistent running game coupled with the Colts' slow start created an underachieving team despite a seventh straight playoff appearance.

2009 Season[xxxi]

The big news heading into the 2009 season was that there was a new head coach for Manning as Dungy retired and gave way to Jim Caldwell, who was promoted from quarterbacks coach after being designated as head coach in waiting during the 2008 season. There would be little, if any, difference for Manning given his absolute command of the offense.

Peyton and the Colts started unevenly, holding off Jacksonville and rallying past Miami to win their first two games. After that, Manning and the team found their groove as they once again chased history in the form of a perfect 16-0 record. Manning carved up secondary after secondary, throwing 12 touchdown passes in a four-game span before being held to only one in narrow wins over San Francisco and Houston as the team improved to 8-0.

In Week 10, the Colts had their annual grudge match against the Patriots, and the game did not disappoint in a shootout at the RCA Dome. Manning rallied the Colts from a 34-21 deficit in the final 4:12, hugely aided by the rare gamble taken by Belichick that backfired. Up 34-28 with 2:23 to play, the Patriots had a chance to run out the clock but gained just eight yards on three plays. Worse still, the Colts judiciously used their timeouts, and the game still had not reached the two-minute warning.

Fearing that Manning would march the Colts the length of the field regardless of distance, Belichick opted to go for it on 4th-and-2 from his 28-yard line to keep the ball out of his hands. Brady completed a pass to Kevin Faulk, but he was stopped short of the first down, giving Manning a much shorter field and a full playbook at his disposal. He took full advantage, finding Wayne with a 1-yard touchdown pass with 13 seconds left for a stunning 35-34 win that kept their unbeaten season going.

Indianapolis kept winning, but barely. A late field goal proved the difference in a 17-15 win at Baltimore, and then Manning had to rally the Colts from an early 17-0 deficit for a 35-27 win at Houston. They made quick work of Tennessee and Denver at home to improve to 13-0, and Manning's 65-yard touchdown pass to Wayne with 5:23 left provided the winning margin of a 35-31 victory at Jacksonville.

With two games to spare, the Colts had wrapped up the AFC South title as well as home-field advantage throughout the playoffs. They had a chance to become just the third team in NFL history to go through the regular season unbeaten and the second in three years after the Patriots did so in 2007. Additionally, dating back to the last season, the Colts were riding an incredible 23-game regular-season winning streak and had history in their grasp.

Caldwell and Colts general manager Bill Polian opted away from a potential 16-0 season in favor of keeping their key players healthy. They pulled Manning and the starters midway through the third quarter against the New York Jets, a team fighting for their playoff lives, leading 15-10. New York would eventually rally to win 29-15, giving itself control of its playoff destiny and causing an uproar among the team's fans and football purists who wanted to see the Colts chase perfection.

Manning completed 14 of 21 passes for 192 yards before being pulled, but he toed the company line in support of his coach after the game.

"We tried to score as many points as we could, we put (backup) Curtis Painter in a tough position," he told *The New York Times*. "This was an organizational philosophy that we stuck with. We still had a chance to win the game. Until any player in here is the head coach, as a player you follow orders, and you follow them with all your heart."

Manning played even less in the season finale, a meaningless 30-7 loss at Buffalo. The Colts finished 14-2, atop the division and the conference. The road to the Super Bowl in the AFC would once more go through Indianapolis.

Any concerns about rust in the postseason quickly vanished as Peyton and the Colts disposed of Baltimore 20-3 in the divisional round. Manning threw a pair of second-quarter touchdown passes, one to Austin Collie that capped an eight-minute drive and another to Wayne as part of a two-minute drill. The defense contributed as well by forcing four turnovers, and the outcome was never in doubt in the second half.

The only team standing between Manning and his second Super Bowl appearance was, surprisingly, New York. After scrambling to make the postseason as a wild card following their gifted win in Indianapolis, the Jets won at Cincinnati in the wildcard round and then San Diego the next week to reach the AFC title game for the first time since 1998.

The Jets had a rookie quarterback in Mark Sanchez, whom they protected with a punishing running game and aggressive defense. Still, every defense feels good about itself until they have to face the game's best in Peyton Manning. Yet it was Sanchez who had the better game for most of the first half, taking the Jets to a 14-6 lead on touchdown passes to Braylon Edwards and Dustin Keller.

They would extend the lead to 17-6 with 2:11 to play, but Manning gave the Colts momentum heading into halftime by conducting another virtuoso two-minute drill, hooking up with Collie on a 16-yard TD pass with 1:13 before halftime to make it 17-13.

On his first possession of the second half, Manning went 6 for eight on a 57-yard drive capped by his four-yard scoring toss to Pierre Garcon to give Indianapolis a 20-17 lead. The Colts would not be denied another conference title, scoring 10 points in the fourth quarter for a 30-17 victory and a date opposite the New Orleans Saints in

Super Bowl in Miami. Manning finished with 377 yards and three touchdowns, completing 26 of 39 passes.

The Colts were returning to a place they lifted the Vince Lombardi trophy just three years prior, although Dolphins Stadium had changed names to Sun Life Stadium. It had been less than five years since the city of New Orleans had been ravaged by the effects of Hurricane Katrina, and the resiliency of the city's citizens was reflected in the Saints as a deep two-way bond emerged between head coach Sean Payton and quarterback Drew Brees with the city's fan base.

While the Colts were rampaging through the AFC, the Saints were doing likewise in the NFC. They won their first 13 games behind Brees' high-powered offense, setting a conference record for most wins by a team before a loss. Even losing the final three games did not dampen the enthusiasm around New Orleans as it enjoyed its best season in franchise history with a 13-3 mark. When it came time for the playoffs, Brees and company were more than ready as they walloped defending conference champion Arizona 45-14 in the divisional round and survived Brett Favre and the Minnesota Vikings in the NFC title game, scraping through with a 31-28 overtime victory. Brees threw for 444 yards and six touchdowns without an interception in the two wins while completing 40 of 63 passes.

The game was expected to be a high-scoring affair, more so because it was the first time two quarterbacks who had thrown for 4,000 yards were meeting in the Super Bowl. The Las Vegas oddsmakers installed the Colts as a 4.5-point favorite to win while expecting the teams to combine for at least 57 points.

For all the jitters Manning showed in his first Super Bowl appearance, he exuded a "been there, done that" vibe in his first possession this time. He marched the Colts 53 yards, going 6 of 7 with an array of short passes to set up a 38-yard field goal by Matt Stover to open the scoring. The second possession was even better as he led the Colts 96 yards to paydirt, finding Garcon on a 19-yard touchdown pass to make it 10-0 in the first quarter.

The offense sputtered in the second quarter, but the Colts' defense bailed them out with a goal-line stand. New Orleans, though, would draw within 10-6 by halftime on a pair of field goals, the second a 44-yarder by Garrett Hartley as time expired.

Once more, it was proven that the best way to beat Peyton Manning is by keeping him off the field. Saints coach Payton made a bold and risky decision to start the second half with an onside kick; if the Saints recovered, they could extend their momentum and potentially take the lead. If the Colts recovered, they would be giving Manning a short field and a chance to take a two-score lead with a touchdown. Thomas Morestead successfully squibbed the second-half kickoff, which was recovered by Jonathan Casillas for the Saints at their 44-yard line. Brees would then pick apart the Colts secondary, going 5 for 5 and completing a 16-yard touchdown pass to Pierre Thomas to give New Orleans a 13-10 advantage.

Undaunted, Manning marched Indianapolis 76 yards on the ensuing possession, highlighted by a pair of third-down completions to Dallas Clark to extend the drive. Addai capped the drive by slashing his way in from four yards, and Indianapolis was back on top 17-13. Heatley's third field goal of the game would pull the Saints within one, and the score remained that way after Stover pulled a 51-yard field goal attempt left with 10:39 to play.

Brees took full advantage of the shortened field, leading the Saints 59 yards to regain the lead with a 2-yard touchdown pass to Jeremy Shockey. The two-point conversion, initially nullified but overturned on a replay challenge by Payton, provided a 24-17 lead for New Orleans with 5:42 to play, plenty of time for Manning to guide the Colts to a game-tying touchdown.

And he gave it his best shot, directing the Colts to the New Orleans' 31-yard line with a series of short passes to Garcon and Wayne. On a 3rd-and-5, though, Manning's hopes of a second Super Bowl victory went up in smoke. Saints cornerback Tracy Porter correctly timed Wayne's inside cut and got to the ball before him for not only the interception but a Super Bowl-securing touchdown as he raced 74 yards by Manning and untouched to the end zone.

The result was a 31-17 loss for the Colts. Manning completed 31 of 45 passes for 333 yards, but that interception confirmed the Saints as destiny's darlings and consigned the veteran quarterback to a bitter defeat.

"Made a great play," Manning told ESPN as he still simmered over the costly interception. "Made a great play. The corner made a heck of a play. Very disappointing. Disappointing."

The loss took the luster off Manning's record-setting fourth NFL MVP award after he threw for 4,500 yards and 33 touchdowns in the regular season. Now 1-1 in Super Bowl appearances, it made Manning more determined to get back there again.

2010 Season[xxxii]

Any questions about Manning's determination were sufficiently answered in the 2010 season opener when he set career highs by going 40 for 57 for 433 yards and three touchdowns, but it was not enough as the Colts fell to the Houston Texans 34-24. Next up came "Manning Bowl II" against younger brother Eli and the New York Giants. This game was nowhere near as close as the first one, and Peyton again got the better of his sibling, this time completing 20 of 26 passes for 255 yards and three scores in a 38-14 laugher.

The Colts were 5-2 after avenging their season-opening loss to Houston with a 30-17 home win as Manning threw for 268 yards and two touchdowns, but they dropped four of their next five games. A 38-35 overtime home loss in which Manning was picked off four times dropped Indianapolis to 6-6 and second place in the AFC South, one game behind Jacksonville.

Manning would close the season with a flourish as the Colts ran the table to win the division title. He threw for 991 yards and nine touchdowns with only two interceptions in the four victories. Despite a 10-6 record, Indianapolis still secured the third seed in the AFC and would open the playoffs against the New York Jets in a rematch of last year's conference title game.

Much like previous year, it was a cagey affair. Manning and Garcon hooked up for a 57-yard scoring play as the Colts held a 7-0 lead at halftime. The Jets pulled even in the third quarter only to have Manning lead the Colts on a drive that ended with a 47-yard field goal that provided a 10-7 edge. New York responded with a marathon 17-play, 87-yard drive that consumed nearly 10 minutes of game clock and was capped by LaDainian Tomlinson's touchdown from one yard with 9:59 to go.

Manning got Indianapolis in field goal position twice, and Vinatieri's second field goal, a 50-yarder, gave the Colts a 16-14 lead with 53 seconds left. Manning had done his job, but unfortunately, the special teams and defense did not do theirs. Antonio Cromartie returned the ensuing kickoff almost to midfield, and Sanchez was able to move the Jets to the Colts' 14-yard line with three seconds to play. Nick Folk then booted Manning and Indianapolis out of the postseason, drilling a 32-yard field goal at the gun to give New York a 17-16 win.

2011 Season^{xxxiii}

During the 2011 offseason, Manning underwent what was supposed to be a regular procedure to treat a herniated disc in his neck. What happened, however, resulted in a drastic change in the trajectory of his career. As he recounted in 2013 to The Washington Post, when he tried to prop himself up in bed, his throwing arm could not bear any weight. While the surgeon explained that it would take some time to recover since the disc was pressing on a nerve, Manning's condition improved far too slowly for his liking. Even worse, his ability to grip a football had been compromised.

"If any other part of your body has some weakness you go, 'Well, I can probably manage,'" Manning said. "But when you're a quarterback and it's your right hand, you're certainly concerned far as being able to do your job. That one motion to prop himself up resulted in him re-herniating the disc and Peyton had to undergo a second surgery that he kept largely off the radar.

Further complicating matters for his recovery was that the NFL was technically in a lockout as the owners and players tried to hammer out a new collective bargaining agreement. This meant that Manning was not allowed to talk to the Colts medical staff or use the team's facilities for rehabilitation. And given his celebrity and what was at stake in his career, especially after the undisclosed second surgery, Peyton wanted to go somewhere that no one could find him.

Enter his old Tennessee teammate Todd Helton, who was now in the twilight of his baseball career with the Colorado Rockies. He pitched the idea of Manning coming to Denver for rehab work, which made sense since he would be out of the prying eyes of the public and could consult with the Rockies training staff, which had extensive experience dealing with pitchers' arms and injuries.

Manning and Helton went to an indoor batting practice area in the bowels of Coors Field to make sure they would not be watched. The simple idea of playing catch took a garish turn for the worse as Manning could not even throw the ball five yards. Helton laughed, thinking that it was a joke, and said, "Come on, quit kidding," only for a somber Manning to reply, "Man, I wish I was."

Eventually, Manning would need a third, and ultimately, a fourth surgery to correct his ailments, and the result was him missing the entire 2011 season. As one would expect, the Colts went into a nosedive without him. They signed journeyman Kerry Collins for a veteran presence under center, but he as well as Painter and Dan Orlovsky all struggled as Indianapolis finished an NFL-worst 2-14. In fact, Indianapolis did not win a game until beating Tennessee on December 18 after starting 0-13.

If there was a silver lining for the Colts, it was that they were so bad without Manning that they "earned" the first overall pick in the 2012 draft. And in many ways, it was fortuitous for them because much like when they had the number 1 pick in 1998 and used it on Manning, there was another franchise quarterback who could be selected in Stanford's Andrew Luck, a two-time Heisman Trophy runner-up.

The team was at a crossroads: Would they pay Manning, who was nearing his 36th birthday, his $28 million roster bonus in mid-March, or would they fully commit to a rebuild as they did 14 years ago and draft Luck? In hindsight, the multiple surgeries made the business decision for the Colts very easy. On March 7, 2012, they announced that they were going to cut Manning just days before that bonus kicked in.

To his credit, Manning understood that the Colts made the right business decision and that at the end of the day, the NFL is a business. But the emotion was still raw in his voice as he addressed the media for the first time as someone who was not the quarterback of the only team he had known since graduating from Tennessee.

"Nobody loves their job more than I do. Nobody loves playing quarterback more than I do. I still want to play. But there is no other team I wanted to play for," Manning said as his voice quivered.

But he also looked forward to the process of being a free agent for the first time. At a second press conference in Florida later that day, he admitted his naïveté to the whole situation.

"I have no idea who wants me, what team wants me, how this process works," he said. "I don't know if it's like college recruiting where you go take visits. I mean, this is all so new to me."

Thus, the 2012 offseason turned into the Peyton Manning Sweepstakes, even with all the question marks about his surgeries. Most of those issues, though, were successfully answered as he underwent a battery of physical tests by teams who were interested in his services.

Almost immediately, three front-runners emerged in the Denver Broncos, San Francisco 49ers, and the Colts' divisional rivals, the Tennessee Titans. All three were teams on the upswing as both the Broncos and 49ers had won their respective divisions the previous season while the Titans had just missed the playoffs. While the 49ers had gone 13-3 and reached the NFC title game, quarterback Alex Smith had his limitations and was not a strong deep-ball thrower. The Broncos won the AFC West despite going 8-8, and team president John Elway, himself a former Super Bowl-winning quarterback, was not sold on the idea of Tim Tebow as the team's long-term answer under center.

The whole process from when Manning was cut to when he signed with the Broncos took less than two weeks. Elway and then-Broncos head coach John Fox traveled to Durham, North Carolina, where Manning was rehabbing with his former offensive coordinator at Tennessee, David Cutcliffe, to make sure the veteran quarterback could still make all the necessary throws. While Manning's work ethic is legendary, Cutcliffe also deserves a lot of the credit for helping Manning rebuild his throwing motion as the two worked non-stop for nearly three months to recoup his physical skills post-surgery.

After Elway and Fox left satisfied, the two sides quickly agreed to a contract that was virtually identical to the one Manning had in place with the Colts before him being cut. It would wind up being a five-year deal worth about $96 million but was reportedly more like a series of one-year contracts. Essentially, Manning and the Broncos were working on a year-by-year basis.[xxxiii]

The news sent shockwaves throughout the NFL as it upset the balance of the AFC, and it was noticed by the folks with his former team in Indianapolis. Colts owner Jim Irsay released a statement that the team wished Manning nothing but the best of luck in continuing his Hall of Fame-caliber career that had already produced a record four Most Valuable Player awards and one Super Bowl ring. One thing was for sure: If Manning entered the 2012 NFL season fully healthy, the Broncos were likely a major threat to be a championship contender that might have the best offense in the league with all of the weapons at Manning's disposal.

2012 Season[xxxiv]

The 2012 season opened with Manning donning the unfamiliar colors of Denver's navy blue and orange after 14 seasons with the blue and white of Indianapolis as well as the horseshoe on the helmet. He would face a stiff challenge in his Broncos debut September 9 as Denver hosted the Pittsburgh Steelers. Manning looked like he never missed a snap, let alone a season, as he completed 19 of 26 passes for 253 yards and two touchdowns, including the go-ahead score in the fourth quarter as Denver recorded a 31-19 win. Manning also recorded his 400th career touchdown pass in the win, joining Marino and Favre as the only quarterbacks to reach that milestone.

Like almost every return from an injury, though, there is one step back for every two steps forward. Manning was picked off three times in a 27-21 loss to Atlanta in Week 2, and a fourth-quarter rally fell short in a 31-25 setback to Houston the following game. Peyton was still getting used to his new teammates and vice versa. Eric Decker was a solid wide receiver, but he was not Marvin Harrison. Manning had familiarity with Stokley from his days with the Colts, but the X-factor on this team would be third-year wideout Demaryius Thomas. At 6-foot-3 and 230 pounds, Thomas had all the physical tools but had not put it together in his first two seasons with the Broncos; the 22nd overall pick in the 2010 draft had just 54 catches in his first two seasons. This is where Manning's legendary demands for high standards proved most beneficial. He helped make Thomas a better player on the practice field and then trusted him to perform in games. Denver fell to 2-3 after a 31-21 loss at New England to Brady and the Patriots, but that would be the last time Manning lost in the regular season. Denver reeled off 11 straight wins as Thomas burst onto the national scene with 94 catches for 1,434 yards and ten touchdowns. Decker contributed 85 receptions for 1,064 yards and 13 TDs as Manning easily won the league's Comeback Player of the Year award after totaling 4,659 passing yards, barely missing his career high from 2010, and 37 touchdowns with only 11 interceptions.

More importantly, the Broncos rolled to the AFC West title, winning the division by a whopping six games, and were the number 1 seed in the postseason. Their 13-3 mark matched Atlanta for the best record in the NFL.

But as often is the case, the regular season matters very little in the playoffs. In the divisional round, the Broncos hosted the Baltimore Ravens, a team they beat 34-17 on the road in Week 15 in a game not as close as the final score would indicate. Manning did not have to carry the Broncos in that game, completing 17 of 28 passes for 204 yards and a touchdown while Knowshon Moreno rushed for 115 yards and a score.

This time around, the game was a wild affair. Manning and counterpart Joe Flacco each had two first-half touchdown passes as the teams were tied 21-all at halftime. Trindon Holliday, who had opened the scoring with a 90-yard punt return, then ran the second-half kickoff back 104 yards to give Denver a 28-21 lead. After the Ravens tied the game late in the third quarter, Manning provided a 35-28 advantage after finding Thomas for a 17-yard touchdown pass.

Flacco, though, was undeterred and got a little lucky when Broncos safety Rahim Moore completely misjudged the trajectory of the deep pass he fired to Jacoby Jones. It silenced the Denver crowd as the Ravens tied the game with 31 seconds to play on a 70-yard touchdown pass that became known as "The Mile-High Miracle." It was onto overtime, and the Ravens were able to thwart Manning on two possessions, the second one ending with an ill-advised throw by Manning across the middle of the field Corey Graham intercepted at the Denver 45. Eventually, the Ravens would win the game early in the second sudden death period, sending Manning and the Broncos to an unexpected early playoff exit.

"Yeah, bad throw," Manning conceded post-game to The AP. "Probably the decision wasn't great, either. I thought I had an opening, and I didn't get enough on it, and I was trying to make a play and certainly a throw I'd like to have back."

The Ravens, meanwhile, would eventually emerge as Super Bowl XLVII champions after hanging on to defeat the San Francisco 49ers 34-31.

2013 Season[xxxv]

After such a disappointing end to the 2012 season with the double-overtime loss to the Ravens at home in the playoffs, 2013 was a much better season and postseason for Manning and the Broncos. They took care of some unfinished business and pent-up frustration in the season-opener by demolishing the Ravens 49-27.

Manning tied an NFL record with seven touchdown passes as Demaryius Thomas, Julius Thomas and free agent acquisition Wes Welker each had two scoring catches, while Andre Caldwell caught the other one. Manning finished 27 of 42 for 462 yards, and perhaps most impressive was that five of the seven TD passes were for 23 yards or longer.

That win served notice the Broncos' offense was a force to be reckoned with. Manning guided Denver to a 6-0 start as the team averaged 44.2 points and scored at least four touchdowns in every game. Manning put up other-worldly numbers in this torrid start, completing 74.2 percent of his passes for 2,179 yards and 22 touchdowns with only two interceptions. The other signature victory in that run was outdueling Tony Romo for a 51-48 victory at Dallas on October 6 in which the two quarterbacks combined for 920 passing yards and nine TDs.

While Manning and the Broncos kept winning, they were barreling towards a landmark game on the calendar. Manning would make his first trip to Indianapolis as an opponent for a match against the Colts on national television in Week 7. The former king of Indianapolis Peyton Manning was now taking on his successor Andrew Luck, who had already shown himself plenty worthy of being the number 1 selection after 23 games.

Manning and the Broncos arrived at Lukas Oil Field 6-0 following a 35-19 win over Jacksonville, while Luck had guided the Colts to a 4-2 mark and first place in the AFC South. For all of the kind words Irsay and Manning had when they parted ways 18 months prior, Irsay kicked off a war of words leading up to the game, noting that the Colts were better suited to build a team capable of winning in the postseason without Manning and his salary. He referred to his former quarterback's regular-season statistics as "Star Wars numbers."

This, in turn, led to an uncharacteristically feisty retort from Fox, who is considered one of the most vanilla coaches in the NFL when it comes to his dealings with the media. The Broncos coach said that Irsay's statements "sounded a little ungrateful and unappreciative to me for a guy that has set a standard, won a Super Bowl, won division titles, and won four MVP awards. I'd be thankful with that one Super Bowl ring because there's a lot of people that don't have one."

Irsay quickly backtracked from some of his statements via Twitter with more context in that if the Colts had given Manning better defense and special teams they could have won more than one Super Bowl before blaming the media for blowing things out of proportion. It was not as if the game lacked for subplots, and here was an intriguing new one.

As for the game itself, it certainly lived up to its big expectations. It started with a classy tribute video by the Colts to Peyton Manning before the outset of the game. Television cameras showed a young fan with a sign saying "Thanks Peyton But Tonight I'm A Colts Fan."[xxxvi]

Even with the return of Broncos defensive end Von Miller, Luck tore apart the secondary for three first-half touchdowns as Indianapolis took a 26-14 halftime lead. He would add a 10-yard scoring run to extend the lead to 19 points before Manning and the Broncos made a late push to get within 36-30 midway through the fourth quarter.

Denver forced a three-and-out to get the ball back, but Manning was picked off on the next play deep in Broncos territory. The Colts would see the game through and hand the Broncos their first loss, 39-33, overcoming Manning's 386 yards and three TD passes.

But the Broncos bounced back with a 45-21 win over the Washington Redskins on October 27 behind 354 yards and four touchdown passes by Manning, who also had three interceptions. Later in the season, the Broncos and the Chiefs had a pivotal AFC West showdown in Week 13 as the teams sported identical 9-2 records. Manning finished with 402 yards five touchdown passes, outplaying Alex Smith as the Broncos won 35-28 in Kansas City to take control of the AFC West. Manning would close the season with a flourish, throwing for 1,352 yards and 14 TDs with only one interception to lead Denver back to the division title with another 13-3 record.

Manning set single-season NFL records for touchdown passes (55) and passing yards (5,477), though the latter was not official until the Elias Sports Bureau confirmed a 7-yard completion in the Week 17 win over Oakland was, in fact, a forward pass and not a lateral after the season ended.

Peyton was elected the Most Valuable Player again for the fifth time, further adding to his NFL-record haul. Currently behind him are Jim Brown and Hall of Famer quarterback Brett Favre, each of whom was named MVP three times. He also won his third NFL Offensive Player of the Year award and his third NFL passing title.

The Broncos opened the playoffs at home against the San Diego Chargers. After Manning threw two first-half touchdown passes to stake Denver to a 17-0 lead, he killed off the game's final 3:53 by keeping Chargers counterpart Philip Rivers off the field for a 24-17 win that advanced them to the AFC title game.

Once more, Manning would match wits with Belichick, Brady, and the Patriots with a spot in the Super Bowl on the line. If the former games against the Patriots showcased Manning's rocket arm that could dissect any secondary, this game was one that showed the value of lessons learned by a veteran quarterback. Manning took what the Patriots gave him, which was a lot of short passes underneath, and resisted the urge to gamble with risky deeper passes.

Though Denver led only 13-3 at halftime on the strength of one Manning touchdown pass and two Matt Prater field goals, those three scoring drives totaled 33 plays and 229 yards. More importantly, they kept Brady off the field for nearly 14 minutes cumulatively. In the second half, Manning methodically marched the Broncos 80 yards in 13 plays after the second-half kickoff, burning more than seven minutes off the clock before finding Demaryius Thomas for a 3-yard touchdown pass and a 20-3 lead. The Broncos would ease to a 26-16 victory, and Manning finished 32 of 43 for 400 yards to return to the Super Bowl for the third time, a journey infinitely sweeter given how close he had been to having his career ended barely two seasons prior.

"We've definitely come a long way in two years," Manning told The AP after improving to 5-10 lifetime against Brady, but also 2-1 in AFC title games. "And bouncing back from last year's playoff loss to put ourselves in this position, it definitely feels very gratifying."[xxxvii]

Super Bowl XLVIII pitted a historic offense: the Broncos, who averaged 36.44 points, against a Seattle Seahawks team that led the NFL in scoring defense at 14.61 points allowed per game. Still, many oddsmakers felt that Denver was a strong favorite as well as a sentimental pick with Manning so close to a second Super Bowl title that would further cement his legacy as one of the game's best quarterbacks.

But anything that could have gone wrong for Manning and the Broncos did. The Seahawks and their "Legion of Boom" defense lowered the boom early and often. On the first play from scrimmage, an errant snap in the shotgun formation sailed over Manning's head and into the end zone where Moreno fell on it for a Seahawks safety.

Seattle quickly added two field goals to make it 8-0, and shortly after Kam Chancellor picked off Manning in Broncos territory, Marshawn Lynch scored from one yard to extend the lead to 15. The worst was yet to come on the next possession, as any momentum Manning had built on the drive was snuffed as Cliff Avril deflected a pass intended for Moreno, and Malcolm Smith returned an interception 69 yards to the house. It was 22-0 Seahawks, and the rout was on. The deficit reached 36 points before Manning threw a consolation touchdown pass to Demaryius Thomas on the final play of the third quarter. The more physical Seahawks defense battered the Broncos' playmakers en route to a 43-8 victory that is still considered a stunning upset as well as one of the most thorough beatings in Super Bowl history.[xxxviii] Take nothing away from a Seahawks team that had the right mix of offense with Russell Wilson throwing for 206 yards and two touchdowns, a defense that forced four turnovers, recorded a safety, and had an 87-yard kickoff return by Percy Harvin.

2014 Season[xxxix]

How would 38-year-old veteran Peyton Manning bounce back from the disappointing loss in the Super Bowl? Well, the gunslinger broke more NFL records during his 2014 season with the Denver Broncos. In the season opener on September 7 at home against the Indianapolis Colts, Manning became only the second quarterback along with Favre to defeat all 32 teams in the NFL after throwing for 269 yards and three touchdowns in a 31-24 win.[xl] When asked by the sideline reporter his thoughts on joining the exclusive club, he said, "It means I'm old. Don't tell me stuff like that."

Denver had another win in which Manning was efficient, completing 21 of 26 passes for 242 yards and three touchdowns in a 24-17 win over the Kansas City Chiefs. But that was followed by a 26-21 loss on the road at Seattle in a Super Bowl rematch in which Manning played markedly better with 303 passing yards and two TDs while coming up short.

He quickly regrouped following the bye week against the Arizona Cardinals on October 5, throwing for 479 yards and four touchdowns in a 41-20 win. It also provided two more milestones for Manning as he tied Marino with his 13th career 400-yard passing game and joined Favre as the only quarterbacks to throw for 500 touchdowns by hitting tight end Julius Thomas for a 7-yard strike early in the match.[xli] It would take Manning just two more games to better Favre's NFL standard of 508 TD passes, with the record-setter an 8-yard toss to Demaryius Thomas in the second quarter of the Broncos' 42-17 blowout win over the San Francisco 49ers on October 19. Manning added another to that record with a 40-yard touchdown pass to Thomas in the third quarter. With 500 well in the rear-view mirror and two more full seasons left on his contract, could 600 be in the offering?[xlii]

Denver finished the season by winning six of their last eight games for a 12-4 record and third AFC West title in as many seasons with Manning under center. It was another great year for Manning, who finished with 4,727 passing yards and 39 touchdowns against 15 interceptions. He also completed 66.2 percent of his passes for the year. It was another year and another statistical marvel for a quarterback who was getting close to that age of 40 – a point in the career when almost all quarterbacks were either on the decline or already retired.

Denver finished as the number 2 seed to New England in the AFC, earning a bye and home-field advantage in the divisional round of the playoffs. Manning would make an early playoff exit once more, this time at the hands of the upstart Luck and his former team. Manning staked the Broncos to a 7-0 lead on a 1-yard scoring toss to Demaryius Thomas, but the offense failed to click after that and was held to 288 yards for the game.

Luck, meanwhile, shook off two interceptions by throwing for 265 yards and two touchdowns in a 24-13 victory that was also his first road win in the postseason. Manning finished with 211 yards, but his fumble after being sacked in the second quarter led to a touchdown and a 14-6 deficit that was too much to overcome. The loss had some fans thinking that maybe Father Time had finally caught up to Manning after his 17th season in the league, as Broncos beat writer Mike Klis of the *Denver Post* wrote in a story about the game.[xliii]

2015 Season[xliv]

Only three days after the Broncos lost to the Indianapolis Colts in the AFC Divisional Playoffs round, John Elway, the team's vice president of football operations and general manager, announced that a change was needed. Fox was fired as the head coach of the Broncos despite having led Denver to four consecutive division titles and their 2014 Super Bowl appearance.[xlv] The search to find a successor did not take long. Elway quickly sought out former teammate and quarterback Gary Kubiak and signed him to a four-year contract to be Denver's next head coach after serving as an offensive coordinator for the

Baltimore Ravens. He had previously been the head coach of the Houston Texans.[xlvi]

With the changes in the Broncos coaching staff, the biggest question remaining was about Manning, who did not have the best start to the season during Denver's 19-13 win at home over the Baltimore Ravens on September 13, 2015. The 39-year-old quarterback was sacked four times and completed just 24 of 40 passes for 175 yards. Manning threw an interception to Baltimore's Jimmy Smith, leading to a touchdown that gave the Ravens a 10-9 lead. But Brandon McManus made all four field goals, including ones of 57 and 56 yards in the thin Denver air in the first quarter, to bail out the offense. So did Broncos' cornerback Aqib Talib, who had a 51-yard interception return for a touchdown.

Manning had more success moving on with 256 yards and three touchdowns during a 31-24 win over the Kansas City Chiefs on September 17. This was followed by a 324 yard, two-touchdown effort in a 24-12 win over the Detroit Lions on September 27, 2015. Manning was not putting up some of the gaudy numbers of his early career, but he also did not have to because the Broncos defense was doing its part in helping the team win its first seven games. Denver suffered its first loss of the season in Indianapolis on November 8, when Manning threw a pair of interceptions along with his 281 yards and two touchdowns in a close 27-24 loss.

But Manning's season took an unexpected turn the following week when he was sent to the bench during a 29-13 loss at home to the Kansas City Chiefs on November 15.[xlvii] It was one of the few times Manning was pulled from a game. He had completed just five of 20 passes for 35 yards – enough to allow him to surpass Favre for the NFL's record for career passing yards. Obviously, fans were worried about Manning's abilities, and the loss to the Chiefs just added pressure from folks who wondered if Kubiak would consider letting fourth-year backup Brock Osweiler step in to provide Manning with a chance to heal fully.

Kubiak's response was that Manning was "fine," but the loss to Kansas City said otherwise. A few days after the embarrassing loss, the team announced that Manning was dealing with plantar fasciitis – pains in the heel originating from a tear in his left foot – that was believed to have developed from playing on the artificial turf the week prior in Indianapolis[xlviii]. Team doctors found that Manning was also dealing with sore ribs, and he was ruled out indefinitely. It was the first time Manning missed a game since he sat out the entire 2011 season due to the multiple neck injuries. That meant the Broncos' offense was going to be led by Osweiler, who had thrown just 30 passes in mop-up roles the previous three seasons and starting for the first time since the 2011 Las Vegas Bowl when he was playing for Arizona State University against Boise State.

Osweiler put up decent numbers in his NFL starting debut in Chicago, as he led a four-play, 74-yard touchdown drive in the team's first possession, which ended with a 48-yard pass to Demaryius Thomas. He added a 10-yard touchdown pass to Cody Latimer and finished 20 of 27 for 250 yards in the 17-15 win on November 22. He started in another five games and Denver went 4-2 in his six starts, during which he threw for 1,967 yards, ten touchdowns, and six interceptions while completing 61.8 percent of his throws.

Manning made his first appearance since the injury during the third quarter of the Broncos' 27-20 win over the San Diego Chargers in Week 17. While Manning completed 5 of 9 passes for 69 yards, Osweiler went 14 of 22 for 232 yards with one touchdown and two interceptions. After the game, Kubiak would not publicly recognize that there was possibly a bit of a quarterback quandary in Denver, and he also would not say who would be the starting quarterback for Denver in the playoffs.[xlix] The good thing for Kubiak was that he had two weeks to mull the decision since the Broncos had claimed the top seed in the AFC over New England with their 30-24 win on November 29 behind Osweiler. So how were the Broncos going to contend for a championship? With a good rushing attack and a defense that could win the turnover battle.

In the end, Kubiak went with his veteran warhorse in Manning as his starting quarterback. But it was also clear that the Broncos could not rely solely on Manning to win. That was evident in the divisional round against Pittsburgh in which the defense bent but did not break against Ben Roethlisberger, who threw for 339 yards without a touchdown as the Steelers were forced to kick three field goals after an early touchdown.

That gave Manning time to settle in offensively, and it paid off in the fourth quarter as he engineered a 13-play, 65-yard touchdown drive that ended with C.J. Anderson's 1-yard plunge to give Denver a 20-13 lead with three minutes to play. They would add another field goal in a 23-16 victory to advance to the AFC title game at home against who else but the Patriots.

It was the Broncos' defense that set the tone of this game, limiting Brady and the Patriots to one first down in their first three possessions. Manning methodically marched Denver to a touchdown on his first possession, finding Owen Daniels over the middle for a 21-yard scoring pass to cap an 83-yard drive.

New England would draw within 7-6 after a late first-half touchdown, but Stephen Gostkowski missed the extra point, a play that would loom large later in the game. The defense gave Manning a short field early in the second quarter after Miller intercepted Brady and returned the ball to the Patriots' 16. Manning found Daniels three plays later from 12 yards to make it a 14-6 game.

The teams traded field goals before halftime, and New England drew within 17-12 on a 38-yard field goal by Gostkowski to cap its first drive of the second half. After that, the Broncos defense dug in and harassed Brady to no end as Miller led the charge with one of the best games of his career.

Denver pushed its lead back to eight points early in the fourth quarter, and the defense twice forced a turnover on downs deep in its territory to end New England drives. Manning, though, failed to see out the game before the two-minute warning, and Brady had one last chance to tie the game starting at midfield with 1:52 to play.

He converted a pair of fourth-down passes on the drive, including one to Rob Gronkowski with 12 seconds left for a touchdown that made it 20-18. The game now hinged on the two-point attempt that the Patriots needed to convert to force overtime. But fate smiled on Manning and the Broncos this time as Bradley Roby picked off the pass Brady intended for Julian Edelman, giving Denver the victory and Manning another chance at a second Super Bowl ring.

Manning finished 17 of 32 for 176 yards but he showed plenty of grit and even added a crucial 12-yard run on third down to keep a drive alive in the second half. In the 17th matchup against Brady, it was only Manning's sixth win against the Patriots' franchise quarterback.[1]

The valuable victory over Brady provided Manning a trip to just his fourth Super Bowl to face the younger Cam Newton and the Carolina Panthers. Usually, a team led by Manning in the Super Bowl would have been favored in the championship. But Manning had not played up to his lofty standards for about a year, and the team was being carried by a Broncos defense that looked more like a blue and orange brick wall.

On the other hand, the Panthers were led by a star quarterback in Newton, who had thrown for 3,837 yards and 35 touchdowns while rushing for another 636 yards and ten touchdowns in the regular season, earning MVP honors while leading Carolina to the league's best record at 15-1.

Super Bowl 50 was a game dictated by the defenses as both sides delivered ferocious hits. But Miller and Denver's defense proved to be the better unit, preventing Newton from making plays out of the pocket where he is at his most dangerous. Miller's sack and strip of Newton led to the game's first touchdown as Malik Jackson pounced on the ball in the end zone to give the Broncos a 10-0 lead in the first quarter.

All told, the Broncos forced four turnovers and had seven sacks with 2.5 of them by the Super Bowl MVP Miller. His second sack and strip of Newton, recovered by T.J. Ward gave the Broncos the ball at the Panthers' 4, and Manning handed off to C.J. Anderson three times for the eventual game-sealing touchdown. The veteran quarterback extended the lead to 24-10 with a two-point conversion pass to Bennie Fowler, who is now the answer to the trivia question of "Who caught Peyton Manning's last career pass?"

Manning finished the game 13 of 23 for 141 yards and an interception, and his 56.6 passer rating for the match was his worst of his four Super Bowl appearances and the fourth-worst of his playoff career.

The numbers did not matter in the slightest as he finally hoisted the Vince Lombardi trophy for the second time in his career.[li]

It's funny to consider Manning the underdog in this Super Bowl matchup, but there is a reason he was considered the underdog. However, with a 1-2 record in the NFL championship game during his prime, a Manning who was obviously playing at with declining abilities and injuries that cost him nearly half the season was not the same Manning that accumulated all of the meaningful NFL passing records over his 18-year career. Maybe that was the big reason that there was about to be some news that would follow the Super Bowl victory, and it just did not come immediately after the Broncos earned their dominant win over the Panthers.

Retirement

Only moments after the Denver Broncos defeated the Carolina Panthers in Super Bowl 50 on February 7, 2016, Peyton Manning demurred during the live interviews about whether this victory would be the crowning jewel to complete his 18 years in the NFL. He avoided the questions again after Miller was named the MVP and handed the trophy over to Manning for him to make his comments during the Vince Lombardi Trophy presentation. The folks at CBS were hoping that Manning would have possibly made a decision 30 minutes after telling the television audience that he was going to take some time to reflect on his career while spending time with his wife and children. Oh, and he also publically stated he was going to enjoy a few beers during that period.[lii]

Fans were left wondering when Manning would announce his future in either direction. It is tough for anyone who has pretty much spent his whole life around the sport, starting at a young age with his father, Archie. Of course, Archie had played in the NFL for a couple of different teams before Peyton himself went on to play at the University of Tennessee and then entered the NFL as the first overall pick in the 1998 draft. However, there was speculation around the league, and the fans were talking. Sure, many wanted to see Manning have another run at a Vince Lombardi Trophy by winning a third Super Bowl. It would also give him one more than his younger brother Eli. It is just tough to think that someone who struggled to be healthy during the season leading up to the playoff push would be able to grind out one more season. There were some who likely would have accepted Manning back at the Denver Broncos central headquarters, but with a young quarterback in Osweiler who showed the potential to be the team's future, the Broncos more likely wanted to go in a different direction. In a way, this felt like déjà vu similar to the way that Manning had left the Indianapolis Colts in 2012.

So if Manning were to decide he wanted to continue playing professional football, what teams would be interested? Probably no one who was close to being a Super Bowl contender. Instead, it would be the teams that desperately needed a quarterback, like the Cleveland Browns and the San Francisco 49ers, who were teams also in desperate need of several other pieces to be playoff contenders. But there was not anything official coming from Manning or the team for about a month after Manning won his second Super Bowl. But on March 7, the Denver Broncos made the announcement on their official website that Manning was going to retire with a formal statement at a press conference the next day, which would also feature Kubiak, Elway, and the team's president and chief executive officer Joe Ellis.[liii]

While Elway – who knows something about retiring on top after winning back-to-back Super Bowls with Denver – never set a deadline for Manning to make a decision, the timing of the retirement announcement was coming close to the March 9 start of the NFL calendar. The timing meant that Manning's $19 million salary for the last year of his contract would have to be guaranteed and would have created salary cap issues if Denver wanted to sign the soon-to-be free agent Osweiler to a long-term deal. Granted, Osweiler would later sign a big contract worth $72 million to play for the Houston Texans starting the 2016 season.[liv]

During his press conference on March 8, 2016, Manning talked about how the number 18 was a good number because he retired from the NFL and playing football after 18 professional seasons.[lv] It was a chance to reflect on how he felt that he was a lucky man to meet the legends of the past like Johnny Unitas, along with playing for two great organizations under another legendary quarterback in Elway. He thanked his teammates during his career as well as the five different coaches who helped him become the player and man that he was leaving Denver and professional football – including Jim Mora, Tony Dungy, and Jim Caldwell during his days with the Colts, and then John Fox and Kubiak in Denver. He also revealed that during the week before the Super Bowl that he was asked by his daughter Mosley if the game against the Panthers was going to be his last game, his response was that it would be, and that they both hoped that he would win that trophy.

Near the end of the press conference, he quoted a Bible verse – 2 Timothy 4:7 – which says, "I have fought the good fight. I have finished the race. I have kept the faith." Considering everything that happened and how Manning overcame multiple neck surgeries to win a Super Bowl championship with Denver, no one could deny that he was able to finish his career on his terms and with the best ending that anyone in any sport could have. It is better to go out on top than be carried out by medical staff.

Chapter 4: Manning vs. Manning

These chapters have focused on Peyton Manning, and there has not been much talk about his younger brother Eli, who has also built a name for himself since the San Diego Chargers picked him as the first selection of the 2004 NFL Draft. The Chargers almost immediately traded him to the New York Giants for another quarterback, Philip Rivers, who was the fifth overall selection in that draft after it became apparent that the younger Manning wanted no part of the Chargers organization. It took a couple of seasons before the younger Manning started to fully realize his potential with a trip to Super Bowl XLII in February 2008 and Super Bowl XLVI in February 2012 – both of which were close victories over Tom Brady and the New England Patriots. In retrospect, each of the Manning brothers won two Super Bowls as starting NFL quarterbacks with Peyton going 2-2 in the championship game while Eli went undefeated in his two Super Bowl appearances. It could also be argued Eli has the more impressive Super Bowl victory considering that he denied Brady and the Patriots NFL immortality by ending their perfect season in Super Bowl XLII.

Peyton has the NFL records in passing yards and touchdown passes, but Eli has been in the league for 12 years compared to Peyton's 18. The younger brother does have impressive career numbers, including more than 48,000 passing yards with 320 touchdowns against 215 interceptions. There are some discussions about which Manning brother is the better quarterback in the NFL, and some would say Eli has the edge considering that he has been perfect in his Super Bowl appearances and others would select Peyton because of his statistics. The tiebreaker would usually go to head-to-head matchups in what many football fans called the Manning Bowl. While neither ever played each other in the Super Bowl or NFL playoffs since they remained in separate conferences, they have faced off in three regular-season games.

The first matchup between the two brothers was on September 10, 2006, when Peyton's Indianapolis Colts traveled to East Rutherford, New Jersey, to face Eli's New York Giants for the first game in league history to feature brothers as opposing quarterbacks.[lvi] After a couple of field goals from kicker Adam Vinatieri gave Indianapolis the 6-0 lead, Peyton finished a touchdown drive with a 2-yard pass to tight end Dallas Clark for a 13-7 lead with a little more than two minutes remaining in the first half.

But Eli led a quick touchdown drive that ended with a 34-yard pass to Plaxico Burress. He threw another touchdown pass of 15 yards to Jeremy Shockey in the third quarter, but he also threw an interception to go with his 247 passing yards. The Colts defense won the turnover battle 2-1 and Peyton's team got the narrow 26-21 win.

The game did have some problems concerning officiating as there were ten penalties for the Giants and only three for the Colts. The biggest was a pass interference call that canceled out a first-down play late in the fourth quarter on which replays showed inadvertent contact that should not have warranted a yellow flag, but Peyton had the first win in the sibling rivalry.

About four years later, the two brothers faced off again in what fans called Manning Bowl II on September 19, 2010, this time at Lucas Oil Stadium in Indianapolis, Indiana. But unlike the first game, this was a much different contest, and in a lot of ways, it was no contest. Peyton was near perfect, completing 20 of 26 passes for 255 yards, which featured a 50-yard touchdown pass to tight end Dallas Clark in the second quarter to make the game 14-0. Nearly five minutes after a field goal, Peyton led another touchdown drive of 45 yards in 58 seconds that ended with a 3-yard pass to Austin Collie for a 24-0 halftime lead. The brothers led touchdown drives, but Eli lost two fumbles and threw one interception as the Colts won in a 38-14 rout. The younger brother probably wanted to forget that game, which gave the older brother a 2-0 lead in the Manning rivalry. But the two had a 10-minute conversation in which Peyton let his younger brother know that he loved him and that his team was going to still do well in the NFC East.[lvii] Both teams finished the season 10-6 in 2010. The Colts won the AFC South and advanced to the playoffs while the Giants were second in their division and missed the playoffs.

The two found themselves facing each other on September 16, 2013, in the third Manning Bowl. But this game would be a lot different considering that this was during Peyton's second season playing for the Denver Broncos and part of his first run to the Super Bowl while playing as the quarterback for Denver. The game got off to a slow start with Broncos' running back Knowshon Moreno scoring the lone touchdown in the first half on a 20-yard run. New York kicker Josh Brown kicked three field goals to give the Giants a 9-7 lead, which lasted about a minute before the Broncos drove to New York's side of the field to kick a 42-yard field goal for a 10-9 lead going into halftime. The Broncos added to their lead about six minutes into the third quarter after Peyton led a 53-yard touchdown drive. It was the first of three second-half touchdown drives, as Peyton completed 30 passes for 307 yards and two touchdowns, while Eli struggled again with four interceptions despite throwing for 362 yards. Peyton won the third game in the sibling rivalry, 41-23. After the game, Peyton told reporters that the match felt strange because seeing Eli struggle made it less enjoyable to play in.[lviii]

The only thing missing in this family-friendly rivalry was a chance for the two to compete against each other for a Vince Lombardi Trophy. While Peyton has won all three games in the series known by many fans as the Manning rivalry and Peyton has had many NFL records that the younger brother might not be able to surpass, at least Eli has a chance to top Peyton concerning Super Bowl wins. Eli had signed a four-year contract extension at the beginning of the 2015 season that was worth about $84 million, meaning that he has a few more years to get that third championship.

Chapter 5: What Makes Peyton Manning So Great?

Peyton Manning was without a doubt one of the greatest quarterbacks of all time. Even Bill Belichick, one of the best head coaches in the NFL, admits that Peyton is the best quarterback he has ever faced. Belichick said that he was not just good in a few areas, but he is practically excellent at everything. Peyton Manning was completely humbled by such praise from the coach of one of the most consistently winning teams in NFL history.

Peyton is the only five-time MVP, and his NFL records in almost every major passing category could stand for decades. He has all of the required physical attributes that a quarterback should have. He stands at 6 feet 5 inches tall, allowing him to see deep down the field and make big plays. Besides that, he has one of the best arms in the NFL with laser precision. He is also one of the most obsessive quarterbacks ever, looking at everything he can to become better and never settling for anything less, no matter what records he has broken. And while all of these attributes contribute to his greatness, one of his best weapons is his intelligence.

Peyton Manning knows how to read opponents' defenses like nobody else, the product of extensive film study that dates back to his childhood with his father. He is often able to see exactly what they are attempting to do before the ball is snapped. He analyzes their positions and practically reads their intent all within a few seconds. You can tell that Peyton knows exactly what to do, and even when an all-out blitz occurred, you would see Peyton quickly throw a screen play and gain yards. He would study his opponent's defense before a game, and he would determine all of their weaknesses.

No-Huddle Offense

While other teams have also used the no-huddle offensive system, nobody did it better than Peyton. He has been recognized for running the no-huddle offense since 2001, which was three years into playing for the Colts. In fact, it probably would not be wrong to say that practically every quarterback in the NFL has learned how to maximize their no-huddle offenses from Peyton given his surgical proficiency directing a fast-paced offense. If you watched him, he was screaming out plays, pausing and moving around as if he is making changes, flapping his arms around, tapping players on the shoulder, and stomping his feet. He developed his signature method and mastered the best way to utilize the no-huddle offense to complement his personality and skills.

But how did Peyton do it so successfully? If you watched him in action, you could see that he was reading the defense and making adjustments to his offense at the same time. He would shout out things like "Mississippi" and use sign language to tell his offense what to do. The entire time, Peyton was making split decisions on the fly, adjusting as he saw appropriate. When he made changes, the offense responded accordingly without second thought. That made each offensive play something completely on the fly, meaning that the defense did not know what to expect.

Because of this, the defense was completely confused by Peyton. Sometimes he was not even calling plays. He was just shouting out misdirection to confuse his opponent. However, any defense going against Peyton could not determine what was real and what was not. All they knew was they had better be ready to figure out what to do when the ball was snapped, and fortunately for Peyton, they just could not quite figure it out.

When the phrase "no-huddle offense" enters anyone's mind, the first person they think of is Peyton Manning. While the no-huddle offense has been used for over 100 years, Peyton added an innovative twist. Pretty much all offenses in the NFL use it, but it is most commonly used during a comeback when the clock is their enemy and they need to get the ball snapped and score quickly before time runs out. However, Peyton used it practically throughout the entire game. His purpose was to keep the defense on its toes and utterly confused as to what was coming up next.

Peyton Works Hard Toward Everything

Peyton Manning had one of the strongest work ethics in the NFL. There was even a time that a picture was taken when Peyton was icing an injured foot while watching plays on a tablet. Peyton was an "over–preparer"—he took competitiveness to the next level. You could practically guarantee that, when he faced a defense, he already knew all the players, their formations, and what their weak points were. He studied the defense like nobody else and picked each defense apart by exposing the team's weak points.

Peyton practiced everything. He knew how to get out of the pocket when he was in trouble, how to throw the ball while in motion, and when to throw the ball away. Peyton was not considered a great scrambler by any stretch of the imagination, but everything else he could do better than anyone else in the NFL, and that is because he worked harder than any other quarterback both mentally and physically.

Conclusion

To say that Peyton is naturally gifted is probably only 25 percent correct. While there is no doubt that he has the physique and height advantage that a quarterback needs to be successful, most of his intelligence and athleticism came from his dedication and hard work. He set a new standard in American football. He studied the game so much that it became his life passion. His knowledge of the game was so sharp that he even amazed his coaches. It would not be far-fetched to say, now that Peyton's career as an NFL quarterback is over, that he could become one of the best offensive coaches of all time simply because of his vast intelligence and knowledge of the game.

Chapter 6: Peyton's Obsessive Behavior

Peyton Manning's fame has risen to such a level that he has been in high demand for endorsing products. He has been featured in many commercials, including those for DirecTV, MasterCard, Nationwide Insurance, and Papa John's Pizza. His lengthy spots for DirecTV with his brother Eli, most notably the "Football on Your Phone" in which the brothers are wearing outrageous hairpieces and break into a slow-jam rap, are arguably among the funniest ever created for the company. Love or hate the ads; there is always a Peyton Manning tag line that winds up being remembered. As part of Mastercard's "Priceless" ad campaign, there are various shots of Manning showing up to cheer on people doing everyday things like you would at a football game. One clip of him chanting "Cut that meat!" to a deli sandwich maker spawned an instant internet meme. He also did an ESPN SportsCenter ad with Eli and their father Archie in which the two acted like typical brothers, complete with ear flicks, "wet willies," shoves, and kicks in the posterior while being led on a tour of the Bristol, Connecticut, studios by anchor John Anderson. His ability to make sentences to the tune of the Nationwide Insurance jingle "Nationwide is on your side" resulted in most of the country saying, "Chicken parm, you taste so good," in a sing-song voice.

Peyton Manning also had a spectacular star turn as guest host of NBC's "Saturday Night Live" in 2007. The performance was highlighted by a hilarious mock public service announcement for the charity The United Way in which he played like an NFL quarterback, complete with audibles, signal-checks, and hard-thrown passes while trying to serve as a mentor to children. In fact, Peyton was completely uneasy about hitting kids with the football while on the set. His father Archie told the Shreveport Times that Peyton "didn't want to do it despite it being a Nerf football, but all the parents of the kids in the spot were yelling, 'hit my kid, hit my kid!' off-camera."

From these commercials, many got the sense that Peyton Manning was an incredibly charismatic and personable person. There is no doubt that he is. However, when it comes to playing competitively in football, Peyton is an entirely different beast.

Obviously, you need to be competitive to win big like Peyton. But he took it to a whole different level, on par with other greats in sports such as Michael Jordan. That is why he is considered one of the best quarterbacks ever, breaking some of the most significant NFL records, including most passing yards in a single season, as well as having the most touchdowns in league history. Even more remarkable is the fact that he was able to accomplish these records after enduring a neck injury that many believed would significantly affect his abilities as a quarterback.

Peyton never missed a game until the season he took off for neck and spinal surgery. He has even become great friends with opposing quarterback Tom Brady, bringing out the best in both by picking each other's brains to determine how they can win against their next opponents. Peyton is known to walk the walk and talk the talk. Peyton's former coach, Tony Dungy, recalled that if Peyton said he was going to do something, it was essentially guaranteed that it was going to get done. There was one instance when Peyton was fined over $8,000 for taunting an opponent who fouled one of his receivers. Peyton said that it was "Money well spent." What is even crazier about this is the fact that it was during a pre-season game that would not count against Peyton's or the Broncos' record. By all means, Peyton is extremely passionate about the sport of football, and it is his driving force to being successful in life.

Peyton is never relaxed about his performance and strives to do better. He is never satisfied with what he has already achieved. His drive toward excellence is what makes his offensive line so successful. He aims at motivating the entire team toward success. It can be instantly felt when he takes over the offense and everyone is plugged into action.

Peyton always had one of the strongest work ethics in the NFL. He was always preparing himself for the next game and wanting to be at his best. He simply would not allow anyone to get in the way of it, either. If he felt that a player was not giving his best or not performing the way they should, he was not afraid to let them know. Peyton abhorred what he considered "stupid mistakes," and there were numerous times when he was seen on the sideline yelling at his teammates for committing these faults. That was simply what made him one of the best quarterbacks of all time. He knew how to get his entire team behind him 100 percent of the way.

Peyton was always prepared for greatness, and it all started when he was a child—thanks to his father, Archie Manning. With his father, a former NFL quarterback, Peyton and his brothers Eli and Cooper would start practicing at 4:30 to 5:30 every morning. His father groomed Peyton and his brothers toward having an extremely competitive and winning spirit. Peyton ended up taking it to a whole new level, practically becoming obsessive. But how competitive is he? He is so competitive that he even shocks his coaches.

There was one instance when Peyton arrived at 6:30 in the morning at the Indianapolis Colts headquarters to meet with his offensive coordinator, Tom Moore. They locked themselves into a room, sat down, and watched tapes of all of Peyton's previous offensive plays. They sat there and ran through every scenario. They wanted to see what went wrong, or even if nothing went wrong, how they could perform it even better. They sat there and deciphered every scenario until they could not think of anything else. After a full day, they all went home and came back the next morning at 6:30 to continue analyzing tapes.

What is crazier is that it was Peyton himself that scheduled this. Moore explained that this is Peyton's compulsion. He will do everything in his power to be better. However, in the end, Tom said that this and the other areas that Peyton is obsessive about have made him an even better offensive coach today.

Conclusion

One of the many qualities a good quarterback possesses is being a great leader. Each quarterback achieves this in different ways. While some quarterbacks are incredibly charismatic, optimistic, and friendly, Peyton's primary means of leading his team is through his compulsiveness in being the absolute best you can be. This is not to state that Peyton is not caring or personable, but if you were to ask any player who played with Peyton, he would say that Peyton demanded that everybody play at his absolute best.

Peyton full-heartedly believed that, since he was willing to do his best and give it his all, then everyone else on his team better do the same. If a teammate lacked in this area, then they should expect to hear from Peyton. He was not shy about letting anyone know. In fact, he would do it in front of everyone, whether at training camp in July or even on the sidelines while being broadcast on national television. All of Peyton's team players knew this about him, and they knew that they better do their best or expect to incur the wrath of their quarterback.

Chapter 7: Peyton's Bad Postseason Luck

Peyton Manning had a tremendous winning record during the regular season. On average, during the last 16 seasons that he played in the NFL, he averaged nearly 11 wins during the regular season. This impressive record proves that Peyton is one of the best quarterbacks of all time.

Peyton played for the Colts for 13 years, and he made it to the postseason all but two years, yet the whole time he was there, he reached the Super Bowl only twice and lost once. When playing with the Denver Broncos, he was able to get the Broncos to the Super Bowl twice and lost once.

When it comes to the postseason, it seems odd to find that the numbers are completely different. Peyton Manning was consistently criticized because he just does not appear to win the big games that count. To illustrate, let us look at some stats. Out of 14 appearances in the playoffs, Peyton was only able to make it to the Super Bowl four times, and he won only twice. But to put this in a better perspective, consider that only two quarterbacks, Brady (7) and Elway (5), have made more appearances than Manning's four. Elway lost his first three before winning the last two.

Out of the 14 times that he helped his team make it to the playoffs, they lost the first game nine times, which is a .357 winning percentage. Compare that to his winning percentage in the regular season, which is near .700 of the time. When you compare the numbers, they just do not match up.

Sure, the franchise owners and fans want a great quarterback like Peyton Manning, but most of them do not care that Peyton has the most MVPs or the highest passing yards in a single season. To them, those awards are individual achievements, but they do not necessarily mean that the entire team was successful. Simply put, franchise owners and fans want to win the big games. They want to be Super Bowl champions. Even if the team has a tremendous record and is the top seed in their conference, it does not guarantee anything unless the team delivers in the postseason. For them, it is all about becoming the Super Bowl champs. With only two Super Bowl victories to declare, Peyton fell short of what everyone expected given his ability to reach the postseason consistently.

Thus, the question: why has Peyton Manning been so unsuccessful in the postseason? There have been many instances in which Peyton defeated a team in the regular season and then lost to that team in the playoffs. Peyton is the second quarterback in NFL history to beat all 32 teams at least once, so why does he seem to struggle so hard at winning some of the games that count in the post season?

To analyze the possibilities, we have to consider many other factors in the equation. We especially need to consider the entire team's performance as well as the performance of his opponents in the postseason.

Most of the Games Were Fairly Close

Out of all of the playoff games that Peyton has played, ten were lost by seven or fewer points. Many of these results could be simply the luck of the draw; one simple mistake could cost you the game. However, out of those ten close games, Peyton had only a 2-8 record. While there were times he could be blamed for the loss, there were circumstances in which his teammates made miscues that loomed larger. However, many would criticize Peyton from the simple standpoint that he is the quarterback. Often, a quarterback is given most of the accolades when a team wins and most of the blame when it loses. In this regard, Peyton Manning has been no different than any quarterback who has even taken a playoff snap under center.

His Teammates

It is easy to blame Peyton for the losses in the postseason, but you have to consider the performances of his teammates. Quarterbacks depend highly on their running backs because they help achieve offensive balance and give quarterbacks a break from throwing the ball every play. There have been many instances where the running back's performance also significantly decreased. The defense is also often to blame since they allowed almost 22 points per game in the postseason. This is considerably more than what they gave up in the regular season. However, many are also quick to point out that Peyton as a leader should help his team to perform better overall and he is to blame for not properly motivating his teammates.

When you compare the stats between Manning and Brady, the all-time Super Bowl-winning champ in the postseason, you will see that Peyton Manning averages 283 passing yards to Brady's 253. Additionally, Peyton's completion percentage is barely better by less than one percent. Peyton also has more passing yards per attempt. So the stats tell you that it is not just a single player's performance, but winning the big game requires the entire team to perform better.

The Broncos and Colts Have Terrible Playoff Records

Finally, one question remains. If we were to blame the Colts themselves as being inadequate in the post season, why is it that Peyton seemed to be unsuccessful with the Denver Broncos? Well, the fact is that both teams have not done well in the postseason. Even before Peyton Manning when Elway was the starting quarterback, the Broncos seemed to have a hard time winning the big games. They were able to win only in two of their six trips to the Super Bowl while Peyton Manning has won two out of four. Again considering that Peyton has better stats than Brady, we cannot rule out that the entire Patriots team has been successful because their culture as a team does not rely on Brady to deliver game-in and game-out to have a better than average chance to win. In fact, Belichick may be the best coach in NFL history to maximize the potential of a roster that lacks blue-chip talent amassed in the draft. Remember, while Peyton was the number 1 overall pick in 1998, Brady was the 199th overall selection in the sixth round in 2000. Reverse the quarterbacks and their teams, does anyone doubt Manning would have more than two Super Bowl titles playing under Belichick?

Conclusion

There could be many reasons why Peyton has been so unsuccessful in the post season. However, one thing is for certain, and it is that you cannot blame Peyton for all of his team's shortcomings. He has shown that he has continuously improved and been an all-time great quarterback. There have been quarterbacks that are recognized as being all-time greats without ever winning a Super Bowl, most notably Dan Marino. So when it is all said and done, Peyton can at least claim victory for winning two Super Bowls. However, many critics state that while Peyton is an all-time great quarterback in the regular season, he falls short of being the all-time greatest of all because nothing is more important in the NFL as winning Super Bowl championships for your fans.

Chapter 8: What is Next for Peyton?

Back in September 2015, there were talks about what Peyton Manning would do after he took his last snap – most commonly, he was asked about coaching.

During an interview on the Dan Patrick show, Manning was asked about becoming a head coach or analyst on television for one of the major networks that provide regular coverage of the NFL. But the quarterback replied that he did not think he could become a head coach at his alma mater with the Tennessee Volunteers football program. Manning said no to that, but he did entertain the idea of being the school's quarterbacks coach because he likes teaching football.[lix] But why not be a head coach? Manning explained that being in a position coach might allow him to be under the radar when things go wrong – no one blames the quarterbacks coach when the team loses a big game.

Becoming a football coach is just one thing that people have talked about as a position that Manning could pursue after he finished his football career. Another job that many think he could Manning could do would be a television analyst covering the NFL. Sure, he has made a lot of money and probably does not need the extra paycheck. He is also unlikely to be an athlete who has gambling problems that others suffered from –e.g., Charles Barkley. But Barkley did make a statement not too long ago about how Manning is still at an age where people do not just sit around, and there is a need to find something else to do after those playing days are over.[lx]

Some former quarterbacks have found successful careers in the world of television, whether on a specialty program focused on football news and rumors or on a pre-game or post-game show on one of the major networks. Many legendary quarterbacks entered the world of broadcasting, including former Pittsburgh Steeler Terry Bradshaw and former New York Giants quarterback Phil Simms, who both won Super Bowl championships during their playing careers. Manning could also go a route similar to that taken by former champion quarterback Troy Aikman, who joined Fox Sports as a color commentator after his career with the Dallas Cowboys ended, often working on the A-team with play-by-play man Joe Buck. It is hard to say how Manning would do as part of a commentary team, but it is nothing new for NFL quarterbacks – especially those who can articulate thoughts quickly, have found success, and can provide that credibility to their expert insight.

Chapter 9: Peyton Manning's Legacy

When it comes down to who is the greatest quarterback of all time, nobody can argue that it is not Peyton Manning. Some people have considered Manning to be the Michael Jordan of football, although Jordan consistently won more championships with the Chicago Bulls in the National Basketball Association. His record speaks that he has made himself the all-time greatest.

Even as Peyton has got older, he still has improved in his performance. Although he has decided to retire, you can see that his heart is still in the game. He already has an estimated net worth of over $100 million, so money was not a reason to stay in the sport.

Peyton had to overcome an extremely sensitive neck injury and surgeries that had many people question whether he could perform at the same level he enjoyed most of his career. His passion for the game proved them all wrong. He proved that he not only was the same quarterback after the surgery, but he had even improved.

Peyton is recognized for saving the Indianapolis Colts, a downtrodden franchise that had little success aside from winning Super Bowl V in 1971. Although Indianapolis parted ways with Manning in 2012 and drafted Luck as their new quarterback in a first-round draft pick, Peyton is still highly loved, revered, and adored in Indianapolis. During Peyton's time playing for the Colts, a new stadium was built. Many claim that this stadium would probably have never been built if it were not for Peyton saving the team. Even when Peyton played against the Colts for the first time wearing a Bronco uniform, they gave recognition to Peyton by playing a tribute video before the game. For the Colts, he was the hero who gave them a fighting chance every season and eventually, a Super Bowl championship.

All quarterbacks are usually obsessive and love the sport, but it is doubtful that you can find anyone who is more obsessive about the game than Peyton Manning. He simply takes it to the next level. Some would even argue that he is compulsive to the point that is detrimental. But his compulsiveness is what makes Peyton one of the greatest ever. He simply cannot be number two; he has to be the best there is. His work ethic and love for the game is at a level that no other NFL quarterback can practically compete with.

Even though Peyton has left the field, his future is secured. He has kept himself as being a good role model, meaning that he will be in high demand to endorse products and services, just as Michael Jordan does today. Peyton has created himself as a major brand. Everyone knows who Peyton Manning is, and practically everyone loves him, and nearly everyone hums the Nationwide Insurance theme as a result of him being its pitchman.

In additional, nobody can deny that Peyton has the highest intelligence in the game. Even his offensive coaches could see that he was not your average quarterback. This means that Peyton could potentially coach in the future. Or there is a possibility that he could invest in a franchise, just as John Elway ended up doing after retiring with the Denver Broncos. No matter what, Peyton's future is secure, and he will always be remembered as one of the greatest and most competitive athletes in the sport of American football.

Final Word/About the Author

I was born and raised in Norwalk, Connecticut. Growing up, I could often be found spending many nights watching basketball, soccer, and football matches with my father in the family living room. I love sports and everything that sports can embody. I believe that sports are one of most genuine forms of competition, heart, and determination. I write my works to learn more about influential athletes in the hopes that from my writing, you the reader can walk away inspired to put in an equal if not greater amount of hard work and perseverance to pursue your goals. If you enjoyed *Peyton Manning: The Inspiring Story of One of Football's Greatest Quarterbacks*, please leave a review! Also, you can read more of my works on *Roger Federer, Novak Djokovic, Andrew Luck, Rob Gronkowski, Brett Favre, Calvin Johnson, Drew Brees, J.J. Watt, Colin Kaepernick, Aaron Rodgers, Tom Brady, Russell Wilson, Michael Jordan, LeBron James, Kyrie Irving, Klay Thompson, Stephen Curry, Kevin Durant, Russell Westbrook, Anthony Davis, Chris Paul, Blake Griffin, Kobe Bryant, Joakim Noah, Scottie Pippen, Carmelo Anthony, Kevin Love, Grant Hill, Tracy McGrady, Vince Carter, Patrick Ewing, Karl Malone, Tony Parker, Allen Iverson, Hakeem Olajuwon, Reggie Miller, Michael Carter-Williams, John Wall, James Harden, Tim Duncan, Steve Nash, Draymond Green, Kawhi Leonard, Dwyane Wade, Ray Allen, Pau Gasol, Dirk Nowitzki, Jimmy Butler, Paul Pierce, Manu Ginobili, Pete Maravich, Larry Bird, Kyle Lowry, Jason Kidd, David Robinson, LaMarcus Aldridge, Derrick Rose, Paul George, Kevin*

Garnett, Chris Paul, Marc Gasol, Yao Ming, Al Horford, Amar'e Stoudemire, DeMar DeRozan, Isaiah Thomas, Kemba Walker and Chris Bosh in the Kindle Store. If you love football, check out my website at claytongeoffreys.com to join my exclusive list where I let you know about my latest books and give you lots of goodies.

Like what you read? Please leave a review!

I write because I love sharing the stories of influential people like Peyton Manning with fantastic readers like you. My readers inspire me to write more so please do not hesitate to let me know what you thought by leaving a review! If you love books on life, football, or productivity, check out my website at claytongeoffreys.com to join my exclusive list where I let you know about my latest books. Aside from being the first to hear about my latest releases, you can also download a free copy of *33 Life Lessons: Success Principles, Career Advice & Habits of Successful People*. See you there!

Clayton

References

i "Archie Manning." *Sports-Reference.com*. Sports Reference, LLC. N.d. Web.

ii "Archie Manning." *Pro-Football-Reference.com*. Sports Reference, LLC. N.d. Web.

iii Conway, Tyler. "Cooper Manning's Injury, Aftermath Play Central Role in ESPN's 'Book of Manning.'" *Bleacher Report*. Turner Sports Network. 2013 Sept. 25. Web.

iv Winklejohn, Matt. "Manning brothers lift Isidore Newman." *ESPN.com*. ESPN. 11 May 2010. Web.

v Game notes and statistics from "Peyton Manning." *UTSports.com*. University of Tennessee Athletics. N.d. Web.

vi "1994 Tennessee Volunteers Stats." *Sports-Reference.com*. Sports Reference, LLC. N.d. Web.

vii Game notes and statistics from "Peyton Manning." *UTSports.com*. University of Tennessee Athletics. N.d. Web.

viii Game notes and statistics from "Peyton Manning." *UTSports.com*. University of Tennessee Athletics. N.d. Web.

ix "1997 Citrus Bowl." *UTSports.com*. University of Tennessee Athletics. 1 January 1997. Web.

x "1996 Heisman Trophy Voting." *Sports-Reference.com*. Sports Reference, LLC. N.d. Web.

xi "Danny Wuerffel." *Sports-Reference.com*. Sports Reference, LLC. N.d. Web.

xii Game notes and statistics from "Peyton Manning." *UTSports.com*. University of Tennessee Athletics. N.d. Web.

xiii Sallee, Barrett. "Classic SEC Football: Tennessee Tops Auburn in the 1997 SEC Championship Game." *BleacherReport.com*. Turner Sports Network. 24 August 2012. Web.

xiv "1998." *OrangeBowl.org*. Capital One Orange Bowl. N.d. Web.

xv "Peyton Manning." *UTSports.com*. University of Tennessee Athletics. N.d. Web.

xvi "Peyton Manning." *Sports-Reference.com*. Sports Reference, LLC. N.d. Web.

xvii "Ryan Leaf." *Sports-Reference.com*. Sports Reference, LLC. N.d. Web.

xviii Freeman, Mike. "N.F.L. DRAFT DAY '98; Colts Agonize to the End, Then Pick Manning." *New York Times*. New York Times. 19 April 1998. Print.

xix Game notes and statistics from "Peyton Manning." *Pro-Football-*

Reference.com. Sports Reference, LLC. N.d. Web.

[xx] Game notes and statistics from "Peyton Manning." *Pro-Football-Reference.com.* Sports Reference, LLC. N.d. Web.

[xxi] Game notes and statistics from "Peyton Manning." *Pro-Football-Reference.com.* Sports Reference, LLC. N.d. Web.

[xxii] Game notes and statistics from "Peyton Manning." *Pro-Football-Reference.com.* Sports Reference, LLC. N.d. Web.

[xxiii] Game notes and statistics from "Peyton Manning." *Pro-Football-Reference.com.* Sports Reference, LLC. N.d. Web.

[xxiv] Game notes and statistics from "Peyton Manning." *Pro-Football-Reference.com.* Sports Reference, LLC. N.d. Web.

[xxv] Game notes and statistics from "Peyton Manning." *Pro-Football-Reference.com.* Sports Reference, LLC. N.d. Web.

[xxvi] Game notes and statistics from "Peyton Manning." *Pro-Football-Reference.com.* Sports Reference, LLC. N.d. Web.

[xxvii] Game notes and statistics from "Peyton Manning." *Pro-Football-Reference.com.* Sports Reference, LLC. N.d. Web.

[xxviii] "Manning wins Big One as Colts beat Bears in Super Bowl." *ESPN.com.* ESPN Internet Ventures. 5 February 2007. Web.

[xxix] Game notes and statistics from "Peyton Manning." *Pro-Football-Reference.com.* Sports Reference, LLC. N.d. Web.

[xxx] Game notes and statistics from "Peyton Manning." *Pro-Football-Reference.com.* Sports Reference, LLC. N.d. Web.

[xxxi] Game notes and statistics from "Peyton Manning." *Pro-Football-Reference.com.* Sports Reference, LLC. N.d. Web.

[xxxii] Game notes and statistics from "Peyton Manning." *Pro-Football-Reference.com.* Sports Reference, LLC. N.d. Web.

[xxxiii] "Peyton Manning, Broncos agree to five-year, $96 million deal." *NFL.com.* National Football League. 20 March 2012. Web.

[xxxiv] Game notes and statistics from "Peyton Manning." *Pro-Football-Reference.com.* Sports Reference, LLC. N.d. Web.

[xxxv] Game notes and statistics from "Peyton Manning." *Pro-Football-Reference.com.* Sports Reference, LLC. N.d. Web.

[xxxvi] "Colts capitalize on miscues to hand Broncos first loss of season." *ESPN.com.* ESPN Internet Ventures. 21 Oct. 2013. Web.

[xxxvii] "Peyton Manning, Broncos advance to AFC Championship Game." *ESPN.com.* ESPN Internet Ventures. 13 January 2014. Web.

[xxxviii] Rosenthal, Gregg. "Seattle Seahawks stomp Broncos for Super Bowl win." *NFL.com.* Around the NFL. 2 February 2014. Web.

[xxxix] Game notes and statistics from "Peyton Manning." *Pro-Football-*

Reference.com. Sports Reference, LLC. N.d. Web.

[xl] Breech, John. "Peyton Manning is second QB to beat all 32 teams after win over Colts." *CBSSports.com*. CBS Sports Digital. 8 September 2014. Web.

[xli] Stapleton, Arnie. "Manning's 500th TD leads Broncos past Cardinals 41-20." *CBSSports.com*. CBS Sports Digital. 5 October 2014. Web.

[xlii] Klis, Mike. "Peyton Manning passes Brett Favre for TD record." *DenverPost.com*. The Denver Post. 19 October 2014. Web.

[xliii] Klis, Mike. "Denver Broncos stunned by Indianapolis Colts in home playoff loss." *DenverPost.com*. The Denver Post. 11 January 2015. Web.

[xliv] Game notes and statistics from "Peyton Manning." *Pro-Football-Reference.com*. Sports Reference, LLC. N.d. Web.

[xlv] Legwold, Jeff. "Lackluster finishes rankled Elway." ESPN.com. ESPN Internet Ventures. 14 January 2015. Web.

[xlvi] "Gary Kubiak takes over Broncos." ESPN.com. ESPN Internet Ventures. 19 January 2015.

[xlvii] Cash, Rana. "Peyton Manning benched after throwing four interceptions vs. Chiefs." SportingNews.com. Sporting News. 15 November 2015. Web.

[xlviii] Renck, Troy. "Explainer: Treatment, recovery time from torn plantar fascia." DenverPost.com. The Denver Post. 16 November 2015. Web.

[xlix] Stapleton, Arnie. "Manning leads Broncos past Chargers 27-20." *CBSSports.com*. Associated Press. 3 January 2016. Web.

[l] Reyes, Lorenzo. "Broncos dethrone Patriots, win AFC's spot in Super Bowl 50." *USAToday.com*. USA Today. 24 January 2016. Web.

[li] Prisbell, Eric. "Broncos slam Cam Newton, Panthers to win Super Bowl 50." *USAToday.com*. USA Today. 7 February 2016. Web.

[lii] "Peyton Manning avoids retirement talk after Super Bowl win." *SI.com*. SI Wire. 7 February 2016. Web.

[liii] McLaughlin, Eliott. "Peyton Manning, quarterback for Denver Broncos, to retire." *CNN.com*. CNN Sports. 7 March 2016. Web.

[liv] "QB Brock Osweiler signs $72 million deal with Texans." *USAToday.com*. Associated Press. 10 March 2016. Web.

[lv] "Transcript of Peyton Manning's retirement speech." *ESPN.com*. ESPN Internet Ventures. 8 March 2016. Web.

[lvi] Branch, John. "Colts Defeat Giants, but Battle of Mannings Is a Tie." *NYTimes.com*. New York Times. 11 September 2006. Web.

[lvii] Miller, Randy. "Peyton Manning retires: Reliving the 3 Manning Bowls." NJ.com. NJ Advance Media. 7 March 2016. Web.

[lviii] Miller, Randy. "Peyton Manning retires: Reliving the 3 Manning Bowls." *NJ.com*. NJ Advance Media. 7 March 2016. Web.

[lix] Brinson, Will. "Peyton Manning on if he'd want to be Vols head coach:

'Absolutely not.'" *CBSSports.com*. CBS Sports Network. 3 September 2015. Web.

ix McCarthy, Michael. "Peyton Manning has much to consider before taking a TV job." *SportingNews.com*. Sporting News. 13 March 2016. Web.

Made in the USA
Las Vegas, NV
04 April 2021

20810043R00070